THE LEGACY OF THE VIKING RAGNAR LOTHBROK

Christopher J Robinson

First published by Barny Books

ISBN No: 978.1.906542.07.8

Publishers: Barny Books
                Hough on the Hill
                Grantham
                Lincolnshire
                NG32 2BB

                Tel: 01400 250246
                www.barnybooks.biz

Front cover by Roger McKay

I dedicate this book to my grandsons

William and Finn

THE LEGACY OF THE VIKING RAGNAR LOTHBROK

INDEX

THE LEGACY OF THE VIKING RAGNAR LOTHBROK

INTRODUCTION

This story has been written as close to historical fact as records allow and concerns the Viking king, Ragnar Lothbrok and his sons, during the period 800 to 900AD. Their impact on the history of England, Ireland, Scotland and France was immense. To understand how and why the Viking age developed as it did, one has to chart the development of Europe under the Germanic tribes after the fall of the Roman Empire. The threat posed to the pagan Danes and their Saxon neighbour by the Germanic tribes, unified under the Franks and converted to Christianity, created a bloody backlash which lasted for nearly 300 years. At the time the Danes were taking their revenge by raiding Christian Europe, the Norse tribes to the north had been colonising large areas of Scotland and Ireland. It was the combination of the Danish and Norse forces through the military and political efforts of Ragnar Lothbrok and his sons which led to the conquest and settlement of whole kingdoms.

THE RISING OF THE GERMANIC TRIBES

The Roman army, respecting the military strengths of the Germanic peoples, recruited them as mercenaries, fortifying the River Rhine in a practical policy of containment. In 9AD, the swelling pride of imperial achievement and sense of invincibility carried them over the river, intent on subjugating the Saxon tribes. On a wet September day in the black pine forests of the north, the 17th, 18th and 19th Legions, comprising some 30,000 men led by Quillius Varas, were harried, broken and hunted to annihilation and was where Germanicus, in later years, found the skulls of his compatriots and the eagle imperial standards, nailed to the judgement trees in the Saxons' sacred groves, sacrificed to Wodin and the gods of their fathers.

Herman (Arminius), a former mercenary, had unified the warriors of the Saxon tribes and had lured Varas into the swampy forests of the north where neither the steel wall of Roman infantry could hold together nor cavalry operate. The Romans, heavily armoured and tired, were unnerved by the wild howling of an unseen enemy. Small bands would descend in fury from well prepared ambushes, attacking isolated groups with their spears and stabbing swords, only to disappear again into the forest gloom, leaving behind the quiet moan of the wind through countless leaves. Led on by such provocation and false intelligence, the Romans entered the fortified abatis, known as broti in Northern warfare. These comprised the cutting down of previously partially felled trees so that the boughs fell pointing outwards, and extended over large distances both to the front and flanks of the advance. By the time the Romans had reached the hostile mountains of greenery and twisted timbers, from which sprang a lethal shower of arrows and spears, the Romans retreat was cut off.

Despite the later foray of Germanicus, the Rhine and Danube rivers remained the frontiers of the unconquered Germanic tribes until 376AD. The Ostrogoths pressed by the Huns asked the Roman emperor Valens for permission to cross the lower Danube and settle in Moesia. A few were allowed over the river, but the problem remained, leading to a pitched battle in August of 378AD at Hadrianopolis. The Ostrogoth's allies, the Sarmatian Alans, had charge of the heavy cavalry, riding large horses, and using long lances. It was the cavalry of the Alans that won the day, with the Roman Legions being decisively beaten and the emperor Valens slain.

After sacking Athens in 396AD, Aleric, king of the Visigoths went on to sack Rome in 410AD. The Empire had refused to allow the Visigoths settlement in Noricum, and Aleric's brother, Wallia, then settled the Visigoths in Aquitaine, later taking Spain. With the

Roman garrisons in Gaul thinned by events, the Bergundians were able to settle at Lyons and in the Rhone valley in 405AD. In the winter of 406AD, the Vandals, Suevi and Alans crossed the frozen Rhine and poured into Gaul, and the competition between the Germanic tribes to take Roman territory reached new heights

The Huns with its army led by Attila reached Northern Gaul by 443AD, but spared Paris. The Visigoths, led by Theoderic, formed a coalition with the Salian Franks under Merovech to check the Huns. Being first to reach a defensive ridge on the Catalaunian grassy plains well suited to cavalry, they defeated the Huns forcing their retreat beyond the Rhine, their leader Attila dying in 453AD. The Frankish war bands then set the pace in the conquest of Gaul. Whilst operating as a Roman client, King Clovis, the Grandson of Merevech, exploited the Frank's status as Roman Federatus, eventually founding Francia (France), when he defeated the last Roman general in Gaul in 486AD. Now more influenced by the culture of Rome, King Clovis then set about conquering his rival Franks and tribal cousins. He took a Christian wife, Clotilda and, in the Easter of 496AD, he was baptised at Rheims. He died in his new capital of Paris, after 30 years rule. The conquest of the other Germanic tribes by the Frankish Merovingian dynasty continued, with a kingdom stretching from the north to the Bavarians in the south. By 700AD the empire had begun to fragment and the fortunes of Austrasia, covering North East France and Belgium, began to rise. Charles Martel, the Controller of Austrasia, defeated his rivals to take North West France, Acquitaine and Bergundy. He then went on to conquer the tribes east of the Rhine. The North African Arabs, who had by now taken the Kingdom in Spain established by the Visigoths when, in a three-day battle on the banks of the River Guadalete, Roderic and his army went down before the Arab invaders. The Visigoth's kingdom was reduced to a mountainous rump in the north. In 729AD, the Arabs were striking into Francia heading for the shrine of St. Martins at

Tours, but Charles Martel succeeded in throwing them back at Poitiers in 732AD.

The peak of the power of the Germanic tribes' expansion was consolidated under the Grandson of Charles Martel, Charles the Great, (also known as Charlemagne). He created the Holy Roman Empire stretching from the Atlantic to the Elbe and was anointed emperor by the Pope. The Franks then subjugated the proud Saxon tribes, and threatened their allies the Danes, the reaction to which caused great misery in Europe that did not peak for over one hundred years. Charles the Great pursued a ruthless and merciless crusade against the Saxons. The three main Saxon tribes were situated West of the River Elbe up to the River Rhine where the River Lippe flows into it. East of the River Elbe up to the River Eyder and the Baltic Sea was a fourth Saxon tribe bordering on the lands of the Slavonic people known as the Abodriti, - the natural enemies of the Saxons and Danes.

In 772AD, the Franks first entered the woodland villages and sacred groves of the Saxons in a surprise attack leaving no time to organise resistance and took their stronghold of Eresburg. Penetrating deeper into Saxony they found the sacred tree known as Irminsul and cut it down. In 774AD, Charles the Great went to Italy to support the Pope against the Lombards when, in reprisal, two of the Saxon tribes raided in the Frank's territory. The tribe, who had owned the sacred Irminsul, raided Hesse and, finding the church at Geismar that Boniface had built out of the wood of Thor's oak, they burnt it to the ground. The other tribe went north and burnt the churches east of the River Rhine as far as Deventer in Frisia. Charles the Great, believing in his divine right, gave the order in Council that the Saxons were to be conquered and converted to Christianity by force. Using the might of his Empire against vastly outnumbered Saxon forces, he marched into the Saxon territory. The warriors of the Mark did what they could before escaping into Denmark, leaving the peaceful village inhabitants at the mercy of a brutish army. The Franks left behind two manned forts at Eresburg and Sigesburg by the Rivers Weser and Lippe. The following year, the Saxons rose again, retaking the forts but were repulsed at the River Rhine. The response of the Franks was again to lay waste to the Saxon settlements. Charles the Great felt fully justified in slaughtering all prisoners.

The Danish king, Siegfred, gave sanctuary to the Saxons, but did not give military assistance. A new leader emerged, a Saxon prince called Widukind (child of the forest), who married the Danish king's sister. In 778, Charles the Great led an expedition against the Arabs in Spain but on his return the fearsome Basques fell upon the vanguard and decimated its ranks. The Saxons in their turn destroyed the Frankish garrisons up to the River Rhine but could not take the fort at Deutz nor could they cross the river. Charles the Great on the other hand appointed missionaries in each district to convert the Saxons to Christianity under the threat of death from Frankish spears. Moreover a great sense of injustice arose when he allied with the Slavonic Abodriti to the east, enabling them to enter Saxon lands near to the Danes' Mark, and displacing the Saxon people. The Danes and Saxons had sought no fight with the Franks but now the Danes were threatened directly. The Danes now took military action and the Danewirke defences, stretching across the south of the Jutland peninsular, were strengthened in preparation for attacks on the Holy Roman Empire.

Charles the Great's tyranny continued apace, with a decree that any reluctance to accept the new Christian faith would be met by death. He was so confident of his iron grip on the Saxons that he started conscripting them into his army. Widukind went back to Saxony to prepare his ground and, with the help of the Danes, invaded Frisia, burning the newly built churches, before returning to Saxony to raise an army including those Saxons conscripted into the Frank's army. He defeated a Frankish force at Sundal, before facing the full might of the Franks. Charles the Great, with the certainty of the Crusader, ordered the beheading of four thousand five hundred Saxon prisoners on the banks of the River Alar. The first encounter between Widukind's army and the Franks was indecisive but the second was a resounding defeat for the Saxons. All resistance had now been spent and in 785AD, Widukind and fellow leader Aelfwine agreed to come in and be baptised at Attigny. This ceremony represented to them a humiliating symbol of their final subjection.

Charles the Great's support for Pope Leo III finally resulted in his recognition on Christmas day 800AD when he was crowned Holy Roman Emperor. It was on this day that Ragnar Lothbrok was born and it is here that our story begins, ahead of the firestorms sweeping Europe, which were to follow.

THE LEGACY OF THE VIKING RAGNAR LOTHBROK

Chapter 1

THE REACTION OF THE DANES

The king of the island of Zealand and adjoining territories in Sweden and Norway up to Viken was Sigurdr Hringr whose eldest son was called Ragnar, a sturdy and active boy.

They lived at Heorot, the Great Hall at Leire, on the shores of Zealand. Hrothgar built The Great Hall from which Beowulf and King Hygelac had planned their expeditions and where the sagas of their exploits and its poetry were retold and passed down through the centuries. The island of Zealand is situated to the east of the Danish peninsular of Jutland, and west of the Swedish mainland, controlling the Eyrar-Sund straits, a strategic waterway allowing shipping to move from the inner Baltic Sea into Jotlandshof (Kattegat) and into the North Sea.

The wealth of Zealand was based on its ship-building, the tolls and dues levied on outside shipping, and the exploits of its fleets. As such it was under constant threat from the politics and ambitions of Skania, the adjoining province in Sweden, and from the Jutlanders to the west in Denmark. One skirmish with Skania had caused the death of Sigurdr Hringr's father at the hands of the Swedish King Fro.

News came to the Danish King Gothfrith of the latest injustice visited on his Saxon allies by the Frankish king and Holy Roman Emperor, Charles the Great. He had started the forced repatriation of the Trans-Albiani Saxons living east of the Elbe, to the lands west of the Elbe, giving their territory to the Slavonic Abodriti, thus bringing the Danes' natural enemies close to their borders.

11

Gothfrith called together the Council of War comprising his Jarls and tributary kings, of whom Sigurdr Hringr was one. They sat on the benches around the Great Hall, each resplendent with their steel helmets, swords and spears reflecting the dancing flames from the huge log fires. The king sat where all could see him on a raised wooden platform. With such a large meeting being called, all were eager to hear the king's reasons and decisions.

Gothfrith stood up and with great anger he began his address, "The Franks have started dispossessing the East Saxons of their homelands. They have brought our enemies, the Abodriti, to our borders, and emboldened them through an alliance with their empire. They have reduced our Saxon allies to slavery. This Christian God they forced upon the Saxons on threat of death is a merciless God. They have shown no mercy to their prisoners, beheading 4,500 Saxons on the banks of the River Alar and they have laid waste to all their lands. We must act before we too are weakened by their manoeuvres."

Gothfrith continued his address, "They attacked the Saxons without warning or provocation. Showing contempt for our Gods, they have cut down Thor's oak trees in Odin's sacred groves and used them to build their temples. The Saxon leader, Widukind, the prince of Westphalia and his General, Aelfwine, have been forced to humiliate themselves, bowing down to their Christian God, making oaths of acceptance in response to their priests foreign words and been pushed under the water by them like drowning dogs."

Gothfrith continued in a steely vein, "The Franks will come to know what it means to anger the Danes. We shall attack them throughout their empire from the Atlantic to the Elbe. They will pay for their arrogance when we destroy their temples and kill their priests but first we will destroy their allies, the Abodriti and their King Drasco. Let each king and Jarl detail the number of ships and warriors they

12

can command. Let us assemble our army on Zealand in forty days time before sailing to the River Oder and the Abodriti."

When Gothfrith had finished his address, the assembly let out a mighty roar of approval, and each went away with fire in their heart.

Sigurdr Hringr hosted the gathering fleet of ships and warriors on Zealand. Ragnar, his eight year old, was fascinated to see such a mighty show of force and to sense the air of excitement and expectation. The Sound was full of ships quietly lying at anchor or beached side by side. The crews were camped in their tents ashore, whilst weapons and provisions were loaded on board. Some of the warriors in their chain mail were busy sharpening their axes, spears and swords on the whetstones and there was much banter between the warriors.

The Council of War met to debate their tactics in the Great Hall. It was agreed that the attack should be mounted by both land and sea to entrap their forces between two armies. First they would sail to the northern coast of the Trans-Albiani Saxon territory east of the River Elbe to disembark a land army. This would move southeast towards the River Oder to destroy the fortified settlements before moving up the river to counter any support sent by the Franks. The larger part of the fleet's army would then move west to meet the land army moving towards them. Each king and Jarl was assigned his particular task, the whole being coordinated by King Gothfrith. Sigurdr Hringr was in charge of directing and coordinating the fleet and Gothfrith's nephew, Hemming, was in charge of the land army.

The Danes pursued their plans with great determination. The Abodriti were totally unprepared, feeling secure behind their alliance with Charles the Great, the Holy Roman Emperor. Both of the land armies found the going easy, causing great destruction, whilst the siege of the fortified settlements on the River Oder fell in short order and were burnt to the ground. On meeting up, the armies crossed the River Oder and turned east towards the main settlement where King Drasco resided, taking horses wherever they found them. King Gothfrith left behind a significant force to protect his fleet on the river Oder and to fortify islands in the river against attack by the Franks.

The Danes had moved so quickly that King Drasco had little time to prepare himself before being confronted by a largely mounted army outside his palisade with warriors arriving on foot by the hour. King Gothfrith lost no time in attacking the fortifications on all sides, opening with a black swarm of arrows to sting the defenders with their steely points and to spread a poisonous fear, forcing them back from the palisade. The Danes, fearless for their safety, were up against the palisade lighting fires in those places that their men were not already storming. Soon they were into the fortification, spreading wild fire, fear and chaos. King Drasco died in the fighting.

The Emperor Charles, now in his later years with declining patience, was a tall steely willed man quick to anger. He received the news of the Danish attack at the heart of his empire at Aix-la-Chapelle (Aachen), seething at the thought that the pagan Danes should dare to attack his allies and was determined to crush them. He ordered his forces in Saxony to send assistance, but these could not bring the fight to the Danes. They were too weak to cross the River Oder in the face of the fortified islands and the fleet moored alongside ready to transport the Danes to the enemy position. Stronger forces were sent to follow and, with the Frank's garrisons in Saxony, they fortified themselves with that of the Abodriti army which was still un-bloodied.

King Gothfrith arrived back at his fleet on the Oder and, hearing of the Franks' presence, decided to attack their fortifications. The Franks, hardened and disciplined after years of fighting to expand the empire, proved no easy match. The Danes eagerness to fight and their fearless nature caused the loss of many men during the siege. When Reginald, the nephew of the king was killed leading an assault on the Franks, Gothfrith decided to withdraw into Schleswig, and began fortifying against an attack.

The Emperor Charles brooded on the last unconquered kingdom challenging his will. He believed it was his divine destiny to subject them to his Christian empire, at the point of a sword. With his generals, he began planning a campaign. However his forays into Schleswig were unsuccessful and he was finally dissuaded by the thoroughness of the defences, the practicalities of the forested terrain and with the fallback of the massive Danewirke defences running from coast to coast. He had not given up easily, but was finally persuaded by the mobility of the Danish forces with their large fleets as they were able to disappear to sea and able to beach them on any shore with complete surprise, so that any victory would be transitory.

It later transpired that the Emperor Charles was in a northern port at the mouth of the River Ems with a substantial force. A Danish fleet led by a minor king arrived intent on attack. Charles seeing the fleet beach on the banks of the river quickly mobilised his forces to attack the ships, but the Danes seeing the forces ranged against them, quickly withdrew. Seeing the ships sailing out to sea and thwarted in his wish to attack them, tears of frustration began to run down Charles's face. Eventually he turned to his retainers and said, "Do you know why I weep? I have no fear that these invaders will harm me, but I am grieved that in my lifetime they should have been so near landing on these shores. I feel great sorrow in foreseeing the evils they will inflict on my offspring and their people."

Gothfrith was equally intent on avenging the subjugation of the Saxons and the loss of his men and his nephew to the Franks. He saw the campaign against the Abodriti as only the beginning and he

15

planned his tactics with care. It was two years later that he sent 200 ships to attack Frisia. He ravaged the island offshore before landing on the mainland. The Frisians quickly bought peace with one hundred pounds of silver. Gothfrith knew the Franks would be able to raise large armies from its vast empire given sufficient time but its size meant locations would often have no garrison and were vulnerable to surprise attack.

In 810AD Godfrith finalized his plans to arrive at the emperor's palace gates at Aix-la-Chapelle, the heart of the empire. He raised an army to invade which he assembled in Saxon territory on the banks of the River Elbe. The emperor Charles had been forewarned and brought his forces to a camp where the Rivers Alar and Weser joined, a good defensive position some sixty miles away. Sigurdr Hringr was under the command of King Gothfrith's nephew, Hemming. All were in a high state of readiness.

Amongst Hemming's division was a man called Hundulfr, a bitter man who was the disaffected son of Gothfrith, but unrecognised by the royal line. He resented his lowly status in the army and the fact that Hemming ignored him but, most of all, he resented the king's lack of support for him. Gothfrith was in no hurry to meet the Franks and with a small detachment he went to fly his hawks on the banks of the River Elbe. On retrieving a bird brought down by his hawks, he was taken by surprise when Hundulfr's reason was overwhelmed by hatred and spite. He seized the opportunity to attack him from behind, killing him with one blow from his sword. The king's attendants then killed Hundulfr.

Hemming quickly brought the army back into Jutland in Denmark, seeing a disaster without the leadership of Gothfrith. The Emperor Charles the Great, on hearing of the departure of the Danes, began to weep, saying "Why was I not deemed worthy to see how my Christian army would have made play with these monkeys?"

Charles the Great foresaw the difficulty of facing up to a mobile fleet, capable of invading with complete surprise anywhere on the shores of Europe. As a zealot, he never questioned the morality of his decisions to spill Christian and Pagan blood in the name of Christ and the effect it would have on the sovereign people he attacked. It was left to more persuasive and wiser missionaries to eventually peacefully convert the Nordic people to Christianity. Charles the Great died in 814AD, only 4 years after the death of Gothfrith. The miseries he foresaw being visited on his descendents duly came to pass.

Chapter 2

RAGNAR'S EARLY YEARS

Ragnar was born in the year 800 and raised in the Great Hall of
Heorot. He was influenced by the sagas told by his father's retainers
and was motivated to dream and plan great exploits of heroism. He
was aware of King Hrothgar who had built Heorot some 300 years
before and of his expeditions into the Rhineland and of his nephew
Beowulf whose heroic poetical adventures were passed down by
word of mouth through the centuries. He was also aware of the threat
to Zealand from the mainland Danes and knew how Hrothgar had
repulsed them in 565AD. Ragnar was interested in all the warrior arts
and developed a love of the sea and his father's ships. Sigurdr Hringr,
his father, spent much of his time away, developing his alliances,
preparing his defences, and meeting threats as they arose. It was in
the winter, when campaigning had ended and the sea had started to
freeze, that Ragnar remembered him best seated beside the great
burning fires amongst his retainers, drinking heavily to pass the days
in good humour and banter, whilst the winds whipped the snows
outside into a blizzard and all felt secure and content.

At the age of eight, Ragnar was sent to Viken, the coastal region
south of Vestfold, and close by the mouth of the Oslo Fjord, to live
with his aunt for his own safety in unsettled times. He enjoyed testing
his skills with mock-weapons against his cousins, much to the
concern of his aunt. He also met the young princes of the Vestfold
kingdom, developing relationships that fared him well in later years.

It was in 812AD, when Ragnar heard of the death of his father, killed
defending Zealand from Haraldr and his brother Reginfrid, who took
over Jutland, Zealand, and by tributary Viken. Ragnar's aunt
arranged for him to stay with the princes in Vestfold, fearing
Haraldr's men would seek him out in Viken. However the next year,

King Gothfrith's sons, Horic and his brother, returned from exile in Sweden, and drove out Haraldr and his brother, killing Reginfrid in a counter attack the following year. Safe now to return, at the age of fourteen Ragnar came back to Zealand to claim his kingdom, and in taking on all the responsibilities that entailed, he quickly became a man.

When he was sixteen Ragnar fulfilled his dreams of leading war bands on skirmishes. At this age he was over six feet tall, physically strong and agile. He had a bold and fearless manner, which the warriors respected and which also proved attractive to women. Still 17 years of age, he was campaigning in the Grenland kingdom in Norway with a small force, to counteract the local incursions made into Viken during the instability caused by his father's death. Travelling west they encountered a large force, some of which were mounted. Ragnar, realising he could not outrun them and effectively defend his forces drew up a defensive shield wall on a rocky uprising to await events. Ten riders broke away from the large force and rode towards Ragnar, stopping out of range of Ragnar's spears. To Ragnar's surprise, a woman called out.

"I am Lathgertha from Golerdal in Hadaland, who is your leader?"

Ragnar replied to laughter, "I am Ragnar Sigurdsen of Zealand and Viken. Have you come to challenge me in personal combat?"

Lathgertha responded, "Your men may laugh, but many a surprise comes from a hasty judgement. I shall call you Ragnar Lothbrok." This brought further laughter from Ragnar's warriors. Lothbrok meant hairy breeches, referring to the leather trousers Ragnar wore, with thick fur on the outer skin. This was a nickname he was to carry with him all his life.

Ragnar made a quip in reply, "You may call me what you wish, but before we start to get intimate, tell me what the men of Golerdal are doing in Grenland. Are you allies or enemies?"

"No," said Lathgertha, "but I could ask the same question of the men of Zealand and Viken."

Ragner replied, "We hold no friendship for the men of Grenland, and have come here to repay them in kind."

"Then we can make common cause, for we too have a score to settle," said Lathgertha.

Ragnar replied, "Let us then sit aside on yonder rock, and talk of your plans, for you haven't brought such a force into Grenland to harass a few farmers."

Ragnar and Lathgertha joined each other. She was no ordinary woman. He estimated her age at about 25 years, and that she had endured many physical demands, creating a strong broad back and arms well capable of combat. She carried her height well, being as tall as Ragnar. An ornate handled sword rested in her belt. He also noticed how beautiful she was, with flaxen coloured hair cut down to the shoulders, with a broad even face and large blue eyes. In those eyes the two recognised a mutual attraction, and smiled at each other in recognition of what each had seen. Lathgertha explained that their purpose was to take a well-fortified settlement, in which the main hall of the king was enclosed. She described the layout and how she expected to surmount its defences.

Ragnar thought for a moment and said, "This would cause too great a loss in taking such a settlement without surprise and I suggest that the king's forces should come to us. If my forces harried the surrounding area, then they will come out to confront our smaller force. If you can ensure your forces are undetected, you can attack from their rear, splitting their forces to fight on two fronts."

"That may be difficult," said Lathgertha, "we have some distance to travel and news of our journey may run ahead of us, so we will need to keep within the forests."

"Then let us make a start," said Ragnar, "you instruct your men and I will command mine."

The war bands were fortunate to arrive without detection. The area lent itself to concealment and ambush. Ragnar posted lookouts to report on the activities of the settlement, whilst commencing the harrying of the farmsteads and smaller settlements round about. He let it be known that the men of Viken had come to repay the Grenlanders' destruction in kind, being careful to allow men to escape. Soon Ragnar had word that a force had left the settlement, so he drew up a defensive position with its flanks protected by rocks and trees and looking down from higher ground. When the Grenland force came into view, Ragnar estimated that they were outnumbered by twenty to one, and in confronting them had put a lot of trust in Lathgertha. He formed up his shield wall, with soldiers behind in reserve to replace those who fell. Soon the battle was joined, with Ragnar's war band felling many Grenlanders with little loss of life to Ragnar's men, but as the larger forces pressed home their advantage, and Ragnar's men had become tired with their shields hacked away by axe and sword in combat, their losses began to rise. Ragnar began to think they would be destroyed before Lathgertha arrived with her forces. Soon however, he saw horses riding into the enemy's rear, and recognised Lathgertha as one of the riders showing little fear or hesitation. Behind came her men on foot, running across the hill, so that soon the attack was turned away from Ragnar. Amongst the confusion, he quickly formed his men into a wedge shape for attack, with the Berserkers at the point of the arrow. The surprise attack being pressed home on both fronts soon caused the Grenlanders to weaken and their forces to try to break away. Ragnar and Lathgertha's forces gave no respite to the Grenlanders, and chased their enemy back to the settlement, which they proceeded to storm. The remaining forces in the settlement had been totally unprepared for this surprise event and the settlement was taken.

Ragnar instructed a detachment of his men to commandeer horses to assist the wounded on the battle site and to collect all the discarded weapons. The plunder taken from the settlement was gathered into one place and shared between Lathgertha and Ragnar. Ragnar instructed his retainers on what part of the plunder he was to keep, and told them to share out the rest between his men. He was anxious to begin his journey back to Viken, since the Grenland king had not been captured and he feared the king might be able to raise a second force, to intercept his small band. Lathgertha then asked Ragnar to travel with her to Golerdal, as her guest. Ragnar agreed to go with five of his retainers, instructing his men to make all haste to Viken and with extreme caution.

At Lathgertha's hall in Golerdal, Ragnar and his men were royally entertained and he remained there throughout the summer. During this time, he and Lathgertha had become lovers and a strong alliance was formed. Ragnar sensed that her father Asbjorn (Esbernus) was not entirely happy with their relationship. As the threat of winter snows became imminent, Ragnar thought of his responsibilities and bade farewell to Lathgertha, returning to Viken, before sailing back to Zealand.

It was in 818AD, when Ragnar was visiting his relatives in Viken, that they said it was time he took a queen. They told him of a great beauty called Aslaug, who lived at Spangarheid in the house of Aki the Karl and his wife Grima. Ragnar decided to visit Aki the Karl. They knew of Ragnar and his exploits, and made him welcome at their long house. Aki the Karl arranged a big feast for Ragnar. It was then that Ragnar first saw Aslaug helping to serve the food and drink. He was stunned by her beauty and for once was at a loss for words. Aslaug was sixteen years old and gave off an air of confidence and maturity beyond her years. She was socially adept in dealing with different people and situations, and was competent in all she did. Ragnar knew that a brash display and clever words would not impress Aslaug and he spent the next days getting to know her better. He found it difficult to know what she thought of him and this spurred him on to find a way to impress her. As time went by, he became determined to win her for his queen and decided it was time to tell her of his wishes to ask her father for permission to marry her.

When the occasion arose, Ragnar began, "You must be aware of your growing ability to charm and delight me, but I was silenced by your beauty, as any man would be on first seeing you. However this is not why I have since been driven to seek out your company and to know more of you. Your composure and regal manner has left a deep impression upon me. I seek a queen, and wish to ask the permission of your father for you to be my wife. How do you feel in this matter, for in truth you hide your thoughts well?"

Aslaug responded, "I sense you have spoken sincerely but what do I know of you? I know you are pleasing to my eye, healthy and strong. I know you are a brave and powerful man and have been mannerly and attentive towards me but I know nothing of your constancy as the years might unfold. I am young and inexperienced in such matters and can only be guided by my father's judgement and his wishes."

"That is good enough for me," said Ragnar, "and if your father agrees, we will marry forthwith."

Ragnar went to Aki the Karl and asked for his permission to marry Aslaug. Aki responded, "Ragnar, you have many manly ways and a fortitude of character and I could ask for no better son in law. Indeed you have earned my respect in many ways as you have impressed your followers before me. However, in matters which please a woman's unfathomable heart and the values they see necessary for that of a good husband, I must first discuss this with Grima."

Grima had also been impressed with Ragnar's forthright manner and sincerity, and the marriage was agreed. Ragnar made gifts of gold and silver to Aki and within a week the marriage and celebrations had taken place. Ragnar then left with his bride for Viken and spent several weeks introducing Aslaug to his relations before sailing back to Zealand. By the time Aslaug had reached the great hall of Heorot, she was pregnant.

The kingdom came under dire threat within months of Ragnar's return to Zealand. Haraldr had returned to Jutland with the support of both the Abodrites and Lewis the Pious, Charles the Great's succeeding son. Worst of all situations saw Haraldr allying with the Skanians, causing Ragnar to defend both the eastern and western seaways around Zealand. Ragnar immediately sent a messenger to Viken and to Lathgertha in Hadaland seeking reinforcements. Taking advantage of Haraldr's distraction by Horic and his brothers' forces counter attacking in Jutland and Haraldr's need for time to build up a fleet in Limafjord, Ragnar dealt first with the Skanian fleet. The fleets were evenly matched and both sides lost many men in the sea battles which followed. The Zealanders were finally successful at the battle at Whitby and Ragnar gained possession of many ships.

Reinforcements first arrived from Viken but shortly afterwards, Lathgertha's fleet of 120 ships arrived off Zealand. Ragnar was astounded by the size of the fleet she had managed to raise. It gave him the opportunity to go on the offensive. The combined fleets gathered off the Jutland port of Limafjord which Haraldr had not blockaded due to his confidence in knowing he had the greatest forces. The skill of the Norse and Zealand seafarers made quick work of Haraldr's unprepared fleet, both inside and outside the harbour, and soon the battle was taken into the town and surrounding area. Haraldr, seeing a dangerous situation building up on his flank, sued for peace with King Horic and his brother. It was agreed that Denmark should be split into three kingdoms. Ragnar and his allies took on board the weapons, armour and possessions of the defeated forces and returned to Zealand with many fine enemy ships. Ragnar took no share in the ships and other prizes of war, apart from selective captured ships but gave them to Lathgertha's men and the Vikeningas, the men of Viken from which the name Viking evolved, being grateful for their timely response in saving his kingdom. Ragnar rewarded his men from his own reserves, grateful that he had received the support when needed. Before their departure, he learnt from the Norse that Lathgertha had given birth to Ragnar's son, called Ubbe, and both were well.

Aslaug also gave birth to a son and, being the first born, he was called Eric meaning "ever the king." With threats to his kingdom neutralised, Ragnar could now go off on campaigns for plunder during the summer months, returning in the Autumn before the snows and, each winter, Aslaug would become pregnant. Her second child was a son called Agnar, followed by Ivarr inn beinlausi - Ivarr the Boneless, who was destined to achieve great things. Despite growing into a tall strong man, he was described as boneless because he was lithesome like a snake, with quick powerful reflexes, which he readily displayed in combat. Aslaug's fourth son was Sigurdr ormr i auga - Sigurdr snake in the eye, so named because of the fierceness shown in his blue eyes should his strong determination ever be thwarted, having the personality and power of the Berserker. Other sons were Halfdan, Bjorn Ironside, Rognvaldr and Hvitserkr. Aslaug also gave birth to three daughters.

Ragnar taught his sons never to feel self-pity or to run away from problems, it being an unmanly trait which he would mock as a weakness. Each son would compete against the other as to who had the greater fortitude. He instilled in them a hardy determination, setting them tasks that required a steely physical endurance. His sons became competitive in reinforcing a code whereby they would never display physical or mental weakness for fear of derision. Ragnar encouraged them to associate with the warriors and to be inspired by their tales and those of their heroic ancestors, never to flinch at the threat of death but accepting the hand of fate as it came, of feigr - fey, and the inevitable end of the doomed man.

Ragnar would often start his voyages from Norway, fitting out his ships in Viken and Vestfold. During such a fitting out, he travelled to Golerdal to see Lathgertha and his son Ubbe, taking gifts in appreciation of her support for his kingdom. He told her of his marriage. She was pleased that Ragnar had come to visit her and to see his son Ubbe. Lathgertha's father, Asbjorn was less pleased and showed an undertone of hostility to Ragnar, despite his previous welcome when Ragnar first arrived at Golerdal. In the brooding presence of Asbjorn Ragnar therefore stayed but a week before returning to his fleet at Viken.

Ragnar undertook many campaigns into Russia, Finland, Sweden and Francia, enhancing his reputation as a warrior king, both in joining fleets under other leaderships and as leader of his own fleet. The Viking fleets had sailed up the River Rhine and plundered Dorstadt and, following the Viking's capture of Walcheren, Louis the Pious gave the provinces of Walcheren, Dorstadt and the surrounding districts to Haraldr whilst he still ruled over a third of Denmark, it being a condition that he defended these provinces from the Vikings. However Haraldr had been forced out of his kingdom in Denmark in 827AD by Horic and his brother who together held the other two kingdoms in Denmark, and in consequence Friesland was soon under the control of the Danes. They received a yearly tribute and were able to fit out their fleets in Frisia. The Frankish kings were too weak to rescue the situation.

The Vikings had visited the island of Noirmoutier at the mouth of the River Loire on the west coast of Francia that emptied into the Atlantic Ocean, and they eventually made a permanent base there. In later years, 67 ships of the Vestfoldingas under the over-lordship of the Norse kings of Dublin had entered the river and sacked Nantes. The men of Vestfold had had the support of Ragnar's men from Viken. Viking fleets raided up the River Garonne to the south and attacked Toulouse. These events were just the start of the suffering Francia had to bear as every river was penetrated by successive waves of Viking fleets.

On returning from such an expedition, Ragnar found part of Zealand in revolt against him. His own son Ubbe, who was then 16 years old, had been used by his Grandfather Asbjorn to stir up discontent in Zealand and had control of the southern part of the island. He wished to supplant Ragnar as king with his grandson Ubbe and fermented trouble in any way that he could, distorting the truth to his own ends. Asbjorn had come with a sizeable fleet and in Ragnar's absence he had found some fertile ground, maintaining his ships had saved the kingdom from Haraldr and he had had no proper compensation for his support. He argued that Ragnar was always away and neglected his kingdom.

Ragnar's fleet landed at Leire in the north of Zealand, discharging their cargo, before re-supplying their ships for battle. Ragnar gathered what intelligence he could, learning that the enemy fleet was situated in the small islands to the south of Zealand and they had a foothold in Southern Zealand. Ragnar decided to first deal with the enemy fleet that he found at Gronsund, a narrow gap between Falstr and Mon. The sea was calm looking like glass, with a long lazy swell coming from the north. Leading his fleet, his men rowed hard to build up as much speed as possible, when Ragnar ordered his men to cease rowing and to prepare for battle. The oars were quickly stowed and the men took up their weapons. Once in range, Ragnar brought the ship broadside on to the nearest enemy vessel and his men unleashed a black storm of spears at the enemy. The odd lucky throw proved fatal, but most spear injuries occurred to unprotected arms and legs, which were nevertheless disabling. Ragnar then brought the ship's prow directly towards the enemy ship, ensuring as little exposed area as possible for a counter attack. With the ship still holding sufficient way, he turned it again to come alongside the enemy ship, and Ragnar's men were quickly over the side and on to the enemy deck where they made short work of defeating its crew.

The rest of Ragnar's fleet had joined battle, when Ragnar saw Asbjorn in a ship closest to the island. He soon had his men rowing towards this ship which was also now under oars and coming towards Ragnar's ship, prow to prow. Apart from twenty strong oarsmen nearest the stern, Ragnar had his crew stow their oars and again prepare for battle. Once in range he steered the ship away to starboard when spears and arrows were unleashed at the enemy. He quickly and skilfully brought the ship round to ram the enemy ship square on to the planking for best effect. This caused the planking to split near the water line and water began to enter. Initial fighting took place at the bows, until the ships slowly drifted alongside one another and heavy fighting over the ship's gunwales took place. As the enemy ship took on water it settled lower and lower so that Ragnar's men had the advantage of the higher platform. Soon they were on the enemy deck and victory could be seen as inevitable. Some of the enemy leapt over the side into the water. Ragnar, seeing Asbjorn at the stern, fought his way to him, knocking him to the deck with his shield. Holding his sword to his throat, he called on the few men still fighting for Asbjorn to surrender. The odd one fought on only to be killed but most threw their weapons to the deck and submitted.

Ragnar lifted Asbjorn up by his throat, saying, "The poison you have spread has done you little good and caused the loss of many lives today. Such treachery from one taken to be my ally can be rewarded with only one thing."

Asbjorn replied, "Ubbe was your first born son and you abandoned him and deprived him of his inheritance."

Ragnar replied furiously, "Ubbe's inheritance was in Golerdal, on which I made no claim or condition other than that of an ally. Ubbe is only just of manly age and well recognised by me as my son. I hold no enmity towards him for he has been badly led by a vexatious and devious fool. He shall stay with me and my sons this winter and he shall see where justice and truth lies. For you, my sword shall amply repay you." With that said, Ragnar thrust his sword into his chest.

The body of Asbjorn was held aloft and the crew called out, "Asbjorn is dead, throw down your swords."

Those Zealanders who had been seduced to the enemy cause readily did so but the men of Hadaland, fearing an inevitable death as prisoners, either fought on or attempted to flee in their ships. Ragnar did not pursue those ships that had been able to escape but concentrated on securing the prisoners and taking charge of their ships. He then took his fleet to Zealand, assembling an army to march on south Zealand where the men of Hadaland had formed their base and where Ubbe was located. Ragnar did not want to fight Ubbe's forces, leading to his son's likely death. Instead, he sent a messenger to tell him Asbjorn was dead and to convey Ragnar's intent. Ubbe was asked to surrender his retainers, who in the light of Lathgertha's previous support for him, would be allowed to return to Hadaland without ransom or reprisal. Ubbe would join his half-brothers and remain on Zealand after denouncing the false ambitions of his grandfather. Ubbe, realising his grandfather's plans had led to disaster, being based on guile and a false sense of injustice and realising his father had been exceptionally merciful towards him, accepted the terms.

In 845AD, Ragnar undertook a major campaign into Francia. After a very severe winter, Ragnar was the leader in charge of a fleet of 120 ships, made up of his own and those of King Horic of Denmark. Ragnar's ships had joined up with those of King Horic off Friesland before sailing to the mouth of the River Seine. They navigated up the river to Rouen, which they plundered along with the surrounding region. Ragnar found the river to be in full stream giving greater draft clearance for his ships and making it difficult for attackers to reach them. He decided to proceed on up the river as far as Chalevanne near St. Germains-en-Laye.

Charles the Bald, the son of Louis the Pious, knew of their coming and attempted to raise an army. However the long civil war in Francia between the sons of Louis the Pious had weakened his forces and the loyalties of his nobles. They were prone to take bribes and were unreliable. In the event he was only able to raise a small force.

Charles, on deploying his men, made the mistake of splitting his forces by stationing them on both banks of the river to shadow the fleet as it rowed upstream against the strong current. Ragnar had reached an island in the river, and seizing his chance to attack the weaker force, ordered his men ashore. They very quickly routed Charles' men and many prisoners were taken.

The Danes had seen the Frankish forces as being weak, and easy to panic by attacks from the flank, since they kept no lookouts, nor read the strengths and weaknesses presented by the lay of the land, nor anticipated what might develop. They also had little stamina to withstand hunger and thirst and would soon desert when deprived of their comforts.

Charles' remaining forces were demoralised and began to slink away and Charles, without ships and a stronger force, decided to retreat to safety behind the stone built walls of the Abbey of Saint Denis. Ragnar took his ships to anchor under the walls of Paris, the furthest the Vikings had ever penetrated upstream. There, his men along with their prisoners, disembarked on an island in the middle of the river, where he began to erect gallows. Charles' men, looking down from the walls watched in horror as Ragnar's men began the process of hanging one hundred and eleven prisoners. Seeing the men fall from the gallows one by one, twitching on the end of the rope, caused the morale of Charles and his men to sink to new depths of despair at the realisation of their impotence.

On March 28th 845AD Ragnar's men invaded the city burning and killing with little opposition. They targeted the three monasteries of St Genevieve, St Germains l'Auxerrois and St. Germains des Pres, taking the plunder they found, but much of the treasure had already been taken out of the city. A colourful marble pillar took Ragnar's eye which he ordered to be removed to give to King Horic. Fate then took a hand, for whilst the monasteries were still being plundered, a thick fog descended in mid afternoon, and with great difficulty, the Danes made their way back to the ships. Some got lost and were killed by the Parisians. The Parisians saw this event as the work of God. Ragnar had no such sentiment and continued with his destruction and plundering. At the same time he began negotiations with Charles the Bald to leave Paris on condition seven thousand pounds of silver was paid. This was quickly agreed, but it took many weeks for the silver to be collected, during which time a further misfortune afflicted some of the Danes who had contracted dysentery from the local food they had scavenged.

Whilst Ragnar began to return to Denmark with great treasure and many Christian slaves, severe dysentery began to spread amongst his men and prisoners. On leaving the River Seine, the filthy conditions on board, caused by the illness, made conditions wretched and navigation unsafe. Ragnar's men, sleeping on the hard wooden deck, their stomachs gripped with pain and losing bodily fluids, became weaker and weaker, lying in the misery of their cold wet clothes.

Ragnar was spared the dysentery. However, the misfortune and distress of some of his crewmen and prisoners did not prevent him making raids on the Frank's coastal settlements on the voyage home, before safely bringing his ships back to Denmark.

The Christians saw the fog and the illness as divine intervention, and some of Ragnar's men were similarly awed by events believing that they had travelled to Bjarmaland, a land of mists and magic.

On Ragnar's arrival in Denmark, he first went to present some of the treasure and the marble pillar to King Horic, who was well satisfied. However the illness spread among the Danish citizens, and King Horic began to have second thoughts about the wisdom of the raids. He became susceptible to the Christian claims of divine retribution, particularly that of Lewis the German, the son of Lewis the Pious, who ruled Saxony close by. He opened communications with Lewis the German to return the Christian slaves without ransom along with the treasure he had received. King Horic, seeing the epidemic was continuing to spread amongst the Danes, which he now saw as supernatural, allowed his fears to grow to the extent that he gave an order to execute those who had returned from the raid. The illness subsided shortly afterwards, enforcing the belief that the events were indeed supernatural. Ragnar however held no such thoughts, being pleased to have accomplished a very profitable return with little loss of his men, and was already planning his next campaign. He quickly took his fleet to sea with his treasures, in order to let the King's fears subside, and to be out of harm's way.

From this point on Ragnar's interest was taken by his knowledge of events in Scotland and Ireland, hearing of the rich farmlands settled there by the Norse and the treasures they had won from the monasteries. He was also inspired by the exploits of his sons and began to feel they were more successful in their voyages than he had been, and a sense of rivalry prevailed. This resulted in expeditions that would lead to great achievements for his sons but, in the end, to his own death.

Chapter 3

RAGNAR'S SONS

The two eldest sons, Eric and Agnar, had been given a ship of war by Ragnar and they had full responsibility for its use, being eager to test themselves in the skills of seamanship, leadership, and the arts of war. As Ragnar's sons, they were able to attract a crew ready to follow them, and they had been successful in obtaining tribute from ships passing through the straits, being mainly Swedish cargo ships. The younger brothers were envious of their exploits and impatient for permission to join their older brothers.

Their younger brother, Ivarr the Boneless, was a much more complex and deep thinking person than his brothers, being fascinated by the cult of Odin and the practice of magic. He had become skilled in the writing of runes and had developed a mystic aura, winning the respect of others who saw him as a warrior priest, with supernatural strength and knowledge. He knew how to intimidate and put fear into his enemies and strategically planned his moves with caution, making his decisions without undue haste. His younger brother, Sigurdr Snake in the Eye, was altogether different, acting instantly on instinct and with great sense of purpose. The two brothers complimented one another well.

Eric and Agnar had graduated to land raids and had also been successful in gaining booty for their war band. They undertook a raid into Sweden, leaving a small band to guard the ship and had penetrated about 10 miles inland when they were suddenly confronted by an army led by the Swedish king, Eysteinn beli of Uppsala, who was in the south of the country by chance. King Eysteinn had been forewarned of their presence, reported by men seeing the approach of their ship to the shore. They were outnumbered and without means of escape. Eysteinn's men cut them down without mercy, save two men who had managed to escape back to the ship. From the wounded prisoners, Eysteinn learnt that he had killed the two eldest sons of Ragnar, king of Zealand, and knew there would be a revenge attack, so he sent spies to forewarn him of such an event. This was not long in the coming.

Aslaug heard the terrible news when the ship returned to Zealand, an angry taste for revenge welling up in their mother's mind and that of their brothers. Ragnar was away campaigning in Finland, but the brother's blood was so hot, they could not wait for his return, and took charge of Ragnar's ships remaining in the Sound. The Norse auxiliaries in Viken were called out to support them, which alerted King Eysteinn that an attack was imminent, and he moved his army into Skania. Ivarr the Boneless took charge as the eldest son and, after landing his forces in Skania, Ivarr sent scouts forward on horse to try to locate the enemy, marching northeast in the general direction of Uppsala. The scouts eventually located the army of King Eysteinn moving southeast towards them, and reported this to Ivarr. As the armies progressed towards each other, Ivarr had an enormous bow made for him to enhance his image, and a large shield on which he was to be carried into battle. As they progressed, a herd of cattle was sighted, and Ivarr ordered that those on horse should herd the cattle before them at a marching pace. Once the armies were in sight of one another by the settlement of Whitby, at a place called Ullr-akr - the wool field, Ivarr put his large frame onto the shield and was hoisted aloft by his men, and the army began a slow run forward with a mighty roar which panicked the cattle. King Eysteinn's men saw the cattle running towards them and, with the sight of Ivarr standing towering over his men on the shield, holding his large bow, it was a frightening sight to behold, which made them wonder what was to befall them. The cattle broke up the lines of King Eysteinn's men, and before they could reform, Ivarr's men were in the thick of them. Sigurdr and Ivarr leapt into the enemy ranks like men possessed, boiling with anger to avenge their brothers' deaths. King Eysteinn's men were unable to recover from such an unexpected onslaught, and began to break away, only to be cut down by Ivarr's men.

Once the enemy had been beaten, Ivarr sought the body of King Eysteinn, who was found lying wounded at the rear of his men. Ivarr turned him over onto his stomach and taking an axe, looked up to the sky. Ivarr then said in a deep emotional voice, "Odin, I make this king's sacrifice to you, to avenge the death of my brothers and that of my great grandfather." He then used his axe to cut the ribs of the king away from his spine, before pulling out the lungs in the ceremony called spreading the eagle. King Eysteinn had expired soon after the first blows of the axe had fallen.

Ivarr had his men recover what weapons they could, and said "In recompense I give you free-rein to ravage the settlements we pass on the way back to our ships, but beyond this I have no wish to wage war, for our brothers have been avenged and this land is without a king. I would rather seek an enemy with greater strength opposed to us."

When Ragnar returned, much to the surprise of his sons, he was very angry to hear the news that they had carried out such a revenge attack, commandeering his ships without waiting for his return. He thought his young sons had usurped his authority, risking everything including his kingdom on such a hastily planned venture. This caused friction with Aslaug. His sons' resentment grew to the point of rebellion as they felt they had been poorly repaid for their achievement in slaying King Eysteinn. When emotions had cooled, Ivarr, seeing no future in a split camp, went to Ragnar to broker a peace.

Ivarr began, "We wished to take no power away from you, nor could we do so by simply standing as young men among your hardened warriors, for you have forged them into steel and earned their respect through your actions and alliances over many years. We were driven to act by dark anger on hearing of the death of our brothers, seeing the distress of our mother and sisters, and in such heated circumstances we had failed to consider the consequences to you if such a hasty response should bring defeat."

Ragnar was somewhat mollified but replied, "I understand your part in the victory was not so small but as you achieved success I will let the matter rest."

As relations with his father improved, Ivarr as the eldest approached him to be given a ship. "I wish to earn my way in the world and learn the arts of warfare as you have done and to gain your respect and that of other men," said Ivarr, "as would any son of Ragnar Sigurdsen."

Eventually Ragnar agreed to give a ship to Ivarr, and he and his brothers went down with him to Leire situated on a fjord on the north of Zealand. The long ship was out of the water on wooden logs, its finely hewed oak planks creating graceful lines over its twenty five metre length, and having a finely carved dragon's head at the prow. With a freeboard of 1.5 metres, the ship drew an un-laden depth of only a metre in the water, enabling it to go up the most shallow of rivers. The ship took 20 pairs of oars and the pine mast was lying alongside the ship. The excitement of Ivarr and his brothers at being given such a magnificent ship was contagious and they decided to launch it and step the mast. The leather throng attached to the steering oar was pulled in and secured to keep the oar above the keel to prevent damage. The brothers then pushed the ship over the rollers, launching it into the still blue green waters, the silver bow wave spreading out to shore astern of it and cascading on the rocks. The mast was hauled on board and stepped on the keelson, being secured in the crone and by the stays. The red square sail was attached to the wooden yard and the sheets secured. The brothers shipped the oars, dropped the steering oar deep into the water and were soon rowing down the fjord, encountering a light breeze from the sea. They rowed standing up in a crouched position as they had no sea chests with them to sit on. Their co-ordination was ragged as a result. Enthusiasm overcame the pained position and the fact that so few oars were being used for such a large ship. At the mouth of the fjord, they turned about and raised the sail, the ship responded quickly to the following breeze. Back at Leire, the ship was securely moored and talk ran ahead on the planning of the first expedition and practical matters such as the raising of an experienced crew.

Ivarr was able to raise a crew, mindful that his success and reputation depended on him adequately rewarding them from the booty gained. He took with him Ubbe and Sigurdr and initially took to waylaying cargo and war ships passing through the straits off Zealand. The size of Ivarr's well-manned ship, led most targets to settle by payment or to part with some of their cargo. Where there was resistance, Ivarr would fight for the ship and its cargo. In one such incident, a Swedish ship, bringing back treasure from a raid in Francia, was heavily laden with silver and gold and though undermanned from losses, was not prepared to give anything away without a fight. Ivarr's men were fresh and well prepared and won both the ship and its booty, though they lost eight of their men.

Ivarr had been cautious about instigating land raids because of the uncertainty of the risks, and because he did not have experience or, more importantly, good intelligence on specific opportunities. One profitable line was the capture of slaves, either to ransom or sell. One of his crew, Ingjald, knew of a poorly defended settlement among the Abodrites, though they had larger reinforcements within half an hours march, so speed and co-ordination were important. Ivarr decided he would undertake the expedition and they were able to set sail eastwards into the Baltic Sea under a light wind. As night drew on, most of the crew were able to sleep on the wooden deck, Aslakr was the youngest of the crew on board and the effect of the fresh sea air and the day's exertions saw him go into a deep sleep, despite the hardness of the wood. As the youngest, he tended to be the object of the older crewmen's jokes and, when he woke up the next morning from the warmth of the sun, he found he was the last to arise. The rest of the crew began to complain bitterly about how tired they were, having got no sleep due to Aslakr's snoring. They darkly discussed what they should do about it before deciding that he should sleep under the decking boards, next to the keelson. Aslakr did not initially think they were serious, but the scowls and sombre tones of their deliberations made him think they were indeed.

Ivarr estimated the ship's speed and the distance he had travelled from the last island of Bornholm, and expected to be off the coast where he wished to make landfall by late afternoon. As the coast came closer he began to look for a long spit of land where they would moor the ship. They had sailed past the spit before they realised it followed the line of the coast eastwards, behind which was a large bay. As the sun was still high, Ivarr decided to sail on in case they had been seen and an ambush prepared. He then headed north before turning about back towards the spit where he arrived just before dusk. The ship was moored to heavy rocks they had brought with them and Ivarr left 5 men to guard the ship and to escape to sea if threatened. Ivarr took his men over the sandy spit and marched towards the settlement which was taken by surprise and gave little resistance.

They managed to capture 25 men, woman, and children, who were tied together and escorted back to the ship by 5 crewmen, whilst Ivarr and the others intended to search the buildings. Before they could proceed further, a young boy had slipped the gate on the kru yard, and an angry bull came out to challenge the intruders. After much snorting, it decided to charge at Ingjald, but Ivarr put a spear into its flank causing it to turn towards him. Further spears struck home and it lurched forward before collapsing on its knees. Just then the lookout came running back to say that a large force was close by.

39

Ivarr ordered his men to run back to the ship, anxious not to be caught in a battle on the foreshore. Aslakr, to the amazement of his companions, ran like a hare, flitting over grass and rocks with ease. He arrived back at the ship long before the others. The ship had slipped its moorings and was ready to row out to sea, when the others arrived, chased by a strong force of Abodrites. Gunnr, a large thickset warrior, was the last to arrive, and his tardiness was rewarded with a spear in his lower leg, but he managed to get on board with the aid of the others. The prisoners had been put to the stern of the ship, to discourage hostile spears, and the ship was rowed well clear of the land to the relief and laughter of all concerned.

Ivarr said of Aslakr, "We will call you Snart from now on," meaning swift and fleet of foot.

Ingjald said to much laughter, "since Snart has saved the day, I think he should be allowed to sleep above the decking boards."

Once at sea, Ivarr suggested Gunnr should hold his leg in the sea for a while to clean the wound and Ingjald joked, "He can't do that, Gunnr's leg is so thick, it will steer the ship around in circles."

Gunnr complained that the water was too brackish here, holding more fresh water than salt water and Ivarr responded to much merriment, "Even so, you have another leg and will still be able to hop into battle." For good measure, Ingjald suggested that, given a stick for support, he would make a good shield wall by himself.

Ivarr's reputation as a competent leader continued to grow, with many seasoned warriors wishing to join his crew or to man the other ships in his fleet, a fleet which continued to increase in size with each expedition. Other leaders also approached him to combine his fleet with theirs in order to undertake larger and more daring expeditions. Ivarr was careful with his choices, never wishing to be in a position where his military judgement might be over-ruled by others. Through his contacts with other fleets, his expeditions had taken him on raids into England, Wales and Ireland.

In 841AD, Ivarr had acquired a new ship capable of crewing 100 men. It weighed 35 tonnes and was 72 feet long, 17 feet wide and drawing a 3 foot draft. He had combined his fleet with that of Eric Bloodaxe planning to attack the West Saxons at Portland on the south coast of England. Before sailing, Ivarr went to the Hof, the wooden temple comprising an assembly hall and shrine where images of the Gods were laid out in a half circle, along with an altar supported by a circle of stones at the centre of which was the gold ring of Thor on which solemn oaths were sworn. Ivarr put animal blood in a bowl which he placed on the shrine, first making his sacrifice to Frey, the God of the Sea, and the giver of riches, by sprinkling the blood on the God's image, and on those of his crew present. He then made a sacrifice to Odin to aid him in battle, and to Thor to sustain him on his voyage. Ivarr and his men then went into the assembly hall where animal meat was boiled in a cauldron over the open fire and the meat was eaten with toasts being drunk to the gods for victory. The ceremonies bonded the men together and strengthened their collective will, each taking on the strength of the pack.

On landing at Portland, Ivarr and Eric's forces were confronted by the men of Dorset led by Ealdorman Ethelhelm, but the West Saxons were soundly beaten and Ealdorman Ethelhelm was killed. Ivarr later made attacks in Romney Marsh, London, Rochester and Canterbury, and returned with much treasure that he invested in building new ships to expand his fleet, after rewarding his men.

Ivarr passed on his knowledge and experience to Ragnar on each return home before winter set in. Ragnar recognised that his expeditions were no longer making the same returns as those of his son and resolved to plan his own expedition

Chapter 4

EXPEDITIONS TO SCOTLAND AND IRELAND

Ragnar retained a deep resentment towards Aslaug, after she had defied her husband and had taken sides with his sons against him. His very position as king had been undermined in this act, since it was not uncommon for sons to usurp the kingdom of their father. He had already faced a challenge from Ubbe's grandfather and with his voyages far afield, any resentments could be quickly formed into rebellions. The death of King Eysteinn was not a light matter and could set off invasions from his kin to seek their revenge whilst Ragnar was away and unprepared. As for Aslaug, she was totally preoccupied with the death of her two eldest sons and had no warmth for Ragnar. The resentment left Ragnar feeling isolated and lonely as he became aware that he no longer had the vigour of his sons to rise to their challenge.

Ragnar left for a campaign in Finland that did not yield much of a return, after which he anchored his fleet off Sweden to re-provision and repair his ships damaged in a storm. One morning, Ragnar saw a small band of men and a young woman approaching on the rocky shoreline and he went forward with his men to meet them. A man came forward from the group to ask who they were and what was the purpose of their visit. Ragnar replied that he was Ragnar Sigurdsen, King of Zealand and Viken, and he was repairing his ships.

The man said, "I am Ulf, and I represent Herrandr, a mighty Jarl of this region of Gautland whose land stretches west from Lake Vattern to the west coast of Sweden."

"And who is this lovely rock flower you have brought with you," asked Ragnar. "She is Thora, the daughter of Herrandr who offers you hospitality in his Hall" said Ulf.

Ragnar was cautious fearing a possible trap, and asked, "I know nothing of Herrandr and wonder why your Jarl should wish me to be his guest."

"I will be open," said Ulf, "You are right to be cautious. My Jarl is under threat from his neighbours and seeks an ally. I thought you might be in league with them but I know of your sons and their sacrifice to Odin of King Eysteinn beli of Uppsala. I know you have no need of small alliances with men of limited power."

"Very well," said Ragnar, "if your Jarl needs assistance, he will not mind me bringing my warriors in full armour, to feed at his table and I will listen to his problems." Ulf readily agreed and so a small force was left with the ships whilst the rest went with Ulf to Herrandr's Hall.

During the journey to the Hall, Thora was animated. Ragnar perceived that she had developed a fascination for him whilst he in turn was taken by her vitality and beauty, but he gave her no encouragement. As they approached the Hall, Herrandr's men, seeing such a large armoured force approaching, took up defensive positions, until Ulf went forward to reassure them that they came in peace.

Herrandr was generous in entertaining Ragnar and his men and Ragnar repaid this by agreeing to help subdue the threatening neighbours, albeit after negotiating a generous share of any spoils for himself and his men. And so over the months, the combined forces subdued their opponents one by one, producing a rich return for limited losses. The knowledge that Ragnar was an ally of Herrandr had been a demoralising factor for their enemies, knowing the circumstances of King Eysteinn's death. During the campaigns, both Herrandr and his daughter Thora, had travelled with the combined forces. Thora's company had been a delight to Ragnar with her good humour and continual attention, but he thought nothing further of this.

With his work completed, and some discreet tears shed by Thora, Ragnar set off to return to his ships. After a day's travel, he was suddenly overcome with a deep sense of loneliness and realised how much he missed Thora's company. He gave in to his need and decided to return to the Hall, sending his men back to the ships with the spoils of the campaign and with orders to complete the ship repairs and provisioning. Ragnar asked Herrandr for consent to Thora becoming his wife and Herrandr readily agreed. Ragnar stayed with Thora at the Hall for a further 3 very happy months, feeling young and light hearted again, before reluctantly returning to his men. He promised to return the following spring and, on doing so, buoyed up with great anticipation and excitement, he was heart broken to hear she and a child had died in childbirth.

Ragnar returned to Zealand in deep despair, and realised he had to break out of the black prison before it corroded his will. He had heard of the Norwegian successes in Scotland and Ireland, who in those days were known as the Norse, and decided to lead an expedition there with his sons. Unlike the Danes who targeted Europe, raided and left, the Norse had colonised and settled the lands they had conquered. They had sailed southwest from the west coast of Norway, across the wild seas of the North Atlantic, settling first in Hjaltland, the islands of the sheep, now known as the Shetlands. From there they sailed south to settle in the Orkney Isles, "the islands of the seals," which were separated from northern Scotland by a narrow Sound known as the Pentland Firth. From the Orkneys, they settled Northern Scotland, which they called Sutherland. They then travelled down the west coast of Scotland, settling the offshore Hebridean islands, which they called Sudreyjar - the southern islands. These islands lay off the west coast of northern Scotland, creating a waterway sheltered from the wild Westerly wind of the Atlantic, being cupped between the islands of the Outer Hebrides and those of the Inner Hebrides lying close to the Scottish mainland. From this passageway known as the Minches, it led past the Western Isles, which the Norse settled alongside the Scots, creating a mixed population, known by the Irish as the Gaill Gaedhil. It bordered on the Scottish kingdom of Dal Riada, the Scots having moved from Northern Ireland to secure an uncertain toehold in the land of the Picts. Constrained by the Picts, they also bordered the British kingdom of Strathclyde to the south, a kingdom stretching from Cumbria to the banks of the River Clyde, with their stronghold at Dunbarton. From the Western Isles, the sea route led into the Irish Sea, and the land of the kings of Erin, which the Norse called Iraland.

The settlements had been preceded by raids in the early 800s on the island monastery of Hy - Iona, when the blood of the defenceless monks stained the white sands red, spilt protecting the shrine of their saint, Columba, who had converted the Picts north of Loch Levin and had founded Iona in 563AD. A later raid saw the remaining monks fleeing to Ireland with the sacred bones of Columba. Raids on the west coast of Ireland off the Sligo coast, saw the monastery of Inishmurray destroyed. Later raids fell on Ulster, Munster and Connaught, and by 826AD, the Norse from Vestfold had permanent settlements in Meath. The local leader of the Vestfoldingas in Ireland was Thorgisl who began to carve out a kingdom. In 832AD he ravaged the holy places at Rathlin and Clondalkin, among others. By 837AD he had command of two fleets totalling 60 ships, which entered the Rivers Liffey and Boyne, where strongholds were built. By 841AD they had captured the fortification of Dublin on the River Liffey. Other fortified ports established by the Norse included Hlymrek (Limerick) on the west coast, Veisufjordr (Wexford), Vethrafjordr (Waterford), Kerlingafjordr (Carlingford Loch), and Strangifjordr (Strangford Loch).

Thorgisl had cleverly perceived the enmity between the Irish King Felim of Munster and the Ard-Ri, the High King of Ireland, Njall Caille of the northern O'Neils. A pact was made between Felim and Thorgisl, combining their attacks against the high king whereby Thorgisl took Armagh and carved out a northern kingdom over half of Ireland called Lethcuinn in the year 843AD.

The Norse colonisers based in Dublin which lay on the route to western France, had established themselves as the over-lords for raids in this area. In 843AD, sixty-seven ships sailed from Vestfold under their control, which established a permanent settlement on the island of Noirmoutier, at the mouth of the River Loire. From there, they ascended the river and sacked Nantes. The following year of 844AD, under their leader Asgeir, a fleet sailed south to enter the River Garonne, sailing some 200 miles up the river to attack Toulouse.

In the same year, Thorgisl had sent an emissary to Emir Abderrhamen II of Spain to discuss the trading of silk, leather and clothing for the many slaves under his control. He had heard of the flourishing slave trade by the Arabs in Spain through his contact with the Vikings based on the island of Noirmoutier. The Emir chose the poet, Algazal to travel to Dublin to meet Thorgisl the following year. However, opposition to the Norse had arisen in the form of Maelsechlainn, (Malachy 1st) the High King of Erin, in alliance with Cerball the king of Ossory. In 845AD, Malachy devised a trap to lure Thorgisl into a situation where he was accompanied by a few men, and capable of capture by a small band. The snare of the Irish worked well, and Thorgisl was taken and tied into a sack, which was then thrown into a deep bog at Loch Owel in Meath. Thorgisl struggled wildly in the sack, which floated for a while, before being pushed under by the poles of Malachy's men. In consequence Malachy was also able to briefly take back Dublin in the year 849AD, but the Norse were quick to retake the fortification.

Algazal subsequently arrived from Spain after Thorgisl's death, and was astonished to be greeted by his wife, Ota - the Queen of the Pagans, a Seeress who took the high seat at festivals at Clonmacnoise on the River Shannon midway between Lough Derry and Lough Rae, when people would travel to consult her from far and wide. Algazal met her in Dublin dressed in fine silks of many colours, seated on a high chair, and she handled the discussions with expertise, negotiating a supply of slaves for the costly pottery and fine cloth offered. Algazal was surprised by the confidence and independence shown by the Norse women.

Ragnar fitted out his ships in Viken for his first exploratory voyage, whilst Ivarr prepared his ships in Zealand with his brothers, and his sisters had woven the raven banners under which they would fight, and which would protect them. Grimr, the commander of a fleet based in Frisia, had approached Ragnar to join his expedition. Grimr had earned his reputation as a bluff berserkr, and had been successful in leading raids into Francia. Ragnar was unsure of him as a tactical leader, but on the basis of his reputation and the size of his fleet, agreed terms for his involvement in the venture. The fleets came together off Viken, and Ragnar gave them instructions to keep some ships in sight at all times. He ordered them to follow his lead to head due west on leaving the Skagerrak and entering the North Sea, then sailing a course according to what the direction of the wind would allow. They would ascertain due north at night from the pole star sitting still in the eye of the heavens, and due south from the sun at midday when highest in the sky. They would then know the direction of the wind and on what quarter the wind must be kept in order to sail west. They were to head for the Orkney Isles, entering the Pentland Firth between North Scotland and the islands, before turning north into the sheltered waters known as Scapa Flow between the islands. The wind was strong and cold for the time of year, blowing from the north, which caused them to sail and drift in a South Westerly direction. At night they slept on the hard wooden deck, covered in salt-water spray, and chilled by the cold wind. Those who took the night watch, had no more comfort in the day, but the sea air and activity sent them into a deep sleep for at least part of the time, allowing them to forget their discomfort. Eventually the wind began to veer towards the east, allowing a more westerly course to be taken, and after 10 days they sighted the coast of Scotland. Some of the ships had not been able to keep up with the leaders but Ragnar decided not to wait for the vanguard, and turned north, fearing any delay would cause greater drift from an easterly wind blowing on to a lee shore. As they progressed, sailing as close to the wind as they could, the shore moved relentlessly towards them. Ragnar's concern grew, and he decided to drop the sail and to row due east into the wind. It was many hours before Ragnar detected he was at last moving away from the shore. The crew took turns in rowing throughout the night.

By the morning Ragnar felt they had made enough distance to again sail north. Several of the ships had got into trouble during the night on the lee shore and Ragnar did not know how they had fared getting so close in to a rocky shore where they saw no natural harbour. The following day the coast fell away, and seeing no islands, Ragnar realised it was a headland he had passed and so continued on a northerly course with the wind causing a drift to the west. The wind continued to veer and the next day another headland came into view, which Ragnar sailed towards, with the wind now safely on the steering board quarter. On rounding the headland, the Orkney Isles could be seen, along with a series of whirlpools along the north Scottish coast. A very strong tide was running east through the straits towards them, and Ragnar decided not to enter the Pentland Firth but to continue north, and enter Scapa Flow from the east between the islands, which he successfully accomplished. The fleet arrived over a period of days, but several ships were missing.

On board one of the ships leaving Viken, were two of the youngest members of the crew. One was called Gunnr who had just turned sixteen years of age and one was called Finn, some 3 months younger, and they had teamed up together to become good friends. Finn was powerfully built with a bull neck, a regular rounded face with large blue eyes that dominated his features and fair hair that grew forward rising to a peak. He had an easy- going personality with a ready smile. Gunnar was more serious in nature, very tall but less compact, with a heart shaped face.

For both it was their first expedition and the older members of the crew took time and pleasure in teaching them all the practical skills they would require, a prerequisite for the survival of all on board. Gunnr and Finn had come with no weaponry and had been lucky to be accepted since each man relied on the skills and reputation of his compatriot. They had been given yew bows with flaxen bowstrings and a bundle of arrows, as their means of attack and defence. For anything more, they would have to win it in the field of battle. They took their turn at rowing when it was necessary, sitting on their sea chests where they kept their few belongings and they were sorely driven to keep time with the sinewy arms of the other rowers. Food and water was stowed under the ships planking, and was doled out at regular times. Despite the excitement of the adventure, life was hard for the two as they became wet and cold, waking from fitful sleep on the hard planking and suffering from sea sickness and blisters on their hands and bottoms from the rowing. Being unused to the motion of the ship itself, this further tired them as they strove to balance themselves with their bodies rather than moving their sea legs. They were however made of hardy stuff and kept up their enthusiasm and determination to learn and to gain the respect of the others, and were rewarded with turns on the steering oar under the guidance of the ship's Helmsman. One night, Finn caused the ship to drift off into the trough of the waves and the violent rolling of the ship woke up the sleeping members of the crew who complained angrily making Finn more attentive in future. This aside, both Gunnr and Finn became adept at steering the ship according to the wind and sea currents.

One night they were woken with alarm as the lookout shouted out, "Rocks, rocks ahead," and all leapt up to see the vague outline of towering cliffs ahead through the black night battened down as it was by the leaden clouds. The sound of surf breaking came to their ears as the Helmsman ordered them to drop the sail and man the oars, as he tried desperately to steer the ship to starboard. It was too late however as beam end on to the cliffs, the heaving sea picked up the ship and threw it down onto the granite rocks, with the sickening sound of the wooden planks being stove in, before being lifted up again to be thrown against another rock which stove in the sides. Some struggled to get on to a cliff ledge above the relentless waves before they smashed the ship to pieces, but many did not make it. Some struggled to a skerry just offshore, not wishing to attempt to gain access to the cliff in the dark with heavy waves crashing on to the rocks. Those still clinging to the skerry at daybreak were successful in reaching the cliff ledge clear of the water.

Many of the Orkney jarls were away on expeditions at the time of Ragnar's arrival. Those fighting men who remained realised they were facing a substantial force. On sight of Ragnar's fleet, they had moved their ships away from Scapa Flow into the island bays and were reluctant to start a fight until pressed by Ragnar's men. Ragnar landed his crews on the main island to the north and, finding no challenge, moved towards the nearest settlements, only to find them deserted. As they proceeded into the island, they captured a group of women, children and older men hiding among the coarse grass on the sand dunes. Ragnar quizzed them on who of the Orkney jarls remained on the island and who was their leader. After establishing that their leader was Einar, he sent him a message with one of the men captured.

Ragnar said to him, "Let him know that Ragnar Sigurdsen of Zealand and Viken and his sons have not come to have you harried and plundered but to establish themselves as over-lords of these islands. Should he not come to negotiate terms in peace and free passage, then we will lay waste to these islands."

Ragnar set up camp in an area of natural fortification. In due course, Einar came to the camp with an accompaniment of over one hundred armed men. Ragnar's men heavily outnumbered them.

Ragnar asked him, "Are you your own masters in these islands or do you pay tribute to others?"

Einar replied, "We are our own masters but the kings of Vestfold claim our allegiance, though they have been unable to enforce their claims. Our jarls have harried the coast of Norway for we are a mighty force in these islands and count those living across the firth in Sutherland amongst us."

Ragnar replied, "You are not so mighty as to withstand the ambitions of the island Danes and I therefore give you my terms. I shall set my son Bjorn Ironsides above you as over-lord and you will pay an annual tribute, which we will collect each spring. You will give me your allegiance in my campaigns and I will protect you against the kings of Vestfold." Einar had no option but to accept but he planned to break the agreement when his full force returned and to resist any attempt to collect tribute in the following year.

Grimr later approached Ragnar, mindful of his share in any spoils of the expedition and complained bitterly, "I have not allied my fleet to talk about kingship but to plunder and take what treasure I can find. I will not share in your tribute and I demand recompense."

Ragnar was irritated and replied, "You have not lost one man nor been required to exert yourself in battle. These men are Norse settlers and it will serve us little to burn their homes when they have had time to hide their possessions and sail away their ships. I know the kings of Vestfold well. If they have not subdued these Orkney jarls, then it is likely I will have to subdue them in battle in order to receive any tribute. I may also have to deal with the men of Vestfold. We will find plunder among the Picts and the Irish and you will earn your share then with the blood of your men." Grimr, with undisguised bad temper, conceded to Ragnar's decision but warned that he would not be cheated of his due. Ragnar did not like to be threatened but he kept his own council.

Ragnar moved his fleet into the Pentland Firth, passing the island of Hoy, which they named after its high peaks above all the other islands. The fleet crossed over to the northern shore of Sutherland looking for a suitable place to moor safely. The hazardous currents flowing through the Firth were driven by the wild westerly winds from the Atlantic and caused the waters to funnel between the mainland and the islands. This created a dangerous place for Ragnar's fleet. In the end Ragnar decided to sail east and back out into the North Sea where a sheltered bay lay south of the headland on leaving the Pentland Firth. He safely anchored his ships and, taking his men ashore, worked his way among the Norse settlements along the northern shore of Sutherland. He met little resistance. Most were quick to submit to Ragnar. Returning to his ships, Ragnar sailed his fleet south to challenge the Picts that were settled on the flatter shores around the Moray Firth.

They arrived in the early light and anchored their ships. They heard only the haunted howling of wolves in the hills in the quiet of the morning. Being known as sea wolves they took this as a good omen. Ragnar decided to attack the settlements in order to take the Picts by surprise. He was able to ravage the area, taking the spoils back to the ships before King Murial could organise an effective defence. The Picts, once organised, appeared as a formidable force, heavily outnumbering Ragnar's men.

Secure on the ships, Ragnar was in no hurry to confront them. He chose his battle site carefully. When the right moment arrived, Ragnar landed his men and formed a defensive position on a small hill. The Picts, wearing no armour and heavily tattooed, made a wild charge at Ragnar's shield wall but they were unable to break through Ragnar's lines with their long heavy swords. Having first been thinned by spears thrown during the charge, the Picts were pushed up against the line by their own men's enthusiasm, and Ragnar's men were able to make good use of their axes lobbing them over their shields. The Picts lost many men this way. Their bodies formed an added obstacle to breaching Ragnar's defences. Ragnar in turn lost few men. The fierce Picts did not seem to learn the lesson and continued their forays until the fire in them was exhausted and they retired for the day. Ragnar was able to take the offensive. Over the following two days the Picts were worn down in numbers and determination. Finally Ragnar was able to rout the Picts. In the ensuing pursuit King Murial was killed, but Ragnar had lost his youngest son Hvitserkr. They cremated him along with the other dead Vikings and raised up a large mound of stones and rock and Ivarr carved a rune. They then plundered the area at will for both bounty and provisions. When all was safely stowed on board the ships, Grimr complained, "These Picts have but a few scratty possessions and little gold and silver to reward me and my men." Scratty meant a goblin or something very small. He continued to grumble and a sour atmosphere developed between the two leaders.

Ragnar decided that they would go back through the Pentland Firth and subdue the Norse settled in the islands to the west of Sutherland known as the Hebrides but which they named Sudreyjar. Sailing north to reach the Pentland Firth they saw men waving to them from the shore. Coming closer inshore they saw that they were men from their own fleet. They had been shipwrecked, and were marching north along the coast in the hope of meeting up with Ragnar. Amongst the group were Gunnr and Finn who, with the others, had managed to climb the cliff and had survived on mussels and other sea creatures they could find along with fledgling birds they caught on the cliff tops. The crew had managed to salvage most of the mail shirts that they called brynies along with their weapons so they were not defenceless. Gunnr and Finn were taken in together on another ship with a red sail, strengthened with the diagonal rope latticework fixed forward of the sail. Their new crewmates made them welcome, though one known as Hagni was a silent and surly berserkr. He remained apart from the others.

The voyage to the Hebrides was arduous with strong winds coming in off the Atlantic and, for most of the time, required aching muscles to row the ships against the prevailing elements of wind and tide. Above them towered the massive granite cliffs one thousand feet high, making the men in their wooden boats feel insignificant below Sutherland's awesome sea defences. They rounded the northwest cape which they named the turning point, but which the Saxons corrupted to Cape Wrath, an apt name. As they turned south, the conditions eased and they were able to sail close to the islands. The white sands between the black granite rocks looked out of place as they surveyed the area. They decided to sail into the lee of the main island and entered a large fjord.

They had noticed fires burning on the high points of the island and realised the Norse had been forewarned and had set up beacons. A significant force had gathered on the hilly north side of the fjord, which continued to grow but they showed no sign of wishing to bring a fight to the shore were Ragnar's ships lay. Ragnar realised he had to take ground on the hills before more hostile forces arrived and he decided to split his forces in a flanking movement. Grimr was to lead his forces on one flank and Ragnar his forces on the other. The Norwegian settlers were led by Herthiofr and held their ground as Ragnar's men approached, not knowing whether to split their own forces. Grimr however held his forces back and when Ragnar's men were nearing the brow of the hill, Grimr had his men turn about. Herthiofr seeing the men turn about, led his men in a full downhill charge at Ragnar's men.

Ragnar bellowed out, "Shield wall, give ground slowly."

The first onslaught was contained, but as they backed down the hill, trying desperately to maintain the shield wall, the enemy began to run alongside them to attack them in the flank and from the rear. To prevent a rout, Ragnar shouted, "Flank, flank." Some of his men dropped out of the shield wall to cover their flanks and rear, but the shield wall was weakened and became more ragged. Ragnar's son, Rognvaldr, was on the shield wall, concentrating on the fact that some of the enemy had broken through, when he fell backwards over a rock. Finding himself suddenly outside the wall, he was struggling to get up when he felt the heavy blow of a sword entering his back. He fell with his head down the slope, feeling little pain, but with the brilliant light of the sun in his eyes. He could make out the leaves of a small tree moving in the wind like a swarm of silver bees and all was quiet. As the cold entered his limbs and moved into his body, he wondered when Odin would call him to his hall, and then the darkness moved in to muffle the sun's light.

Ragnar's men held together as best they could, finally arriving back at the ships with many casualties. Knowing they could no longer be outflanked, they held a line on the shore whilst the injured were helped on board by the men left to attend the ships. Ivarr and Sigurdr were prominent in their aggressive fighting, and rallied their men to drive the enemy back, many turning to flee. This gave them time to get into the ships safely on Ragnar's recall, and their discipline had saved them from disaster. Both Gunnr and Finn had not taken part in the fighting, having been left with the group tending the beached ships. Seeing the retreating forces of Ragnar, they had helped push the ships off the beach for a quicker escape, and had had their first opportunity to use their bows in anger, and with some success. The body of Rognvaldr was not recovered, as Ragnar could no longer rely on the support of Grimr, and acting alone his forces were likely to lose more men in trying to recover his body.

Ragnar led his fleet to a small, uninhabited island to the south of the fjord, where he landed his men to eat and rest and to tend the wounded. Sigurdr on seeing Grimr with some of his men strode up to him and shouted in his face, "Kunta, you kunta, you planned to see us all killed." As Grimr reached for his sword, Sigurdr struck him in the face with his axe, breaking his eye socket and upper jaw, finishing with a blow to his neck which almost decapitated him. Grimr's men drew together defensively, their weapons at the ready.

Ragnar immediately called out, "Hold your council. You have lost a leader and I have lost a son. We need no further bloodshed. Those who wish to return can go in peace with their share, and those who wish to stay can do so on the same terms as agreed with Grimr." Grimr's men relaxed and conferred together and, on electing a new leader, called Bullr, they agreed to stay to a man.

When Ragnar felt his men had been sufficiently rested, he took his fleet south between the Hebridean islands. A sea fog developed as they were about to enter the passage. Being aware of the strong uncertain currents and, even though the water was deep, there was the odd low-lying skerry that it would be unsafe to tackle in a fog. They therefore lay to, securing their ships to rocks as best they could. In the night a disorientated robin flew on to Ragnar's ship seeking a place to perch. In the morning the sun quickly burnt off the fog, and the Robin seeing land began to sing with a full heart. The crew took

57

this as a good omen from Thor, since the robin was named after the Red Beard of Thor. The fleet then set sail, the rounded peaks of the islands rising out of the sea like a pod of huge black whales. As they left the Hebrides behind and moved into the Atlantic, the weather was fair with a stiff breeze but a heavy swell continued to roll in on the steering board side, making life on board uncomfortable. Eventually they sighted the north coast of Ireland, altering their course south east to sail down the east coast and into the Irish Sea in the year 849AD.

Ragnar tested the Norse defences penetrating Strangford and Carlingford lochs but found the defences too strong for his depleted forces, with the Norse fortified settlement of Annagassan ten miles to the south of Carlingford loch. He sailed south and saw an opportunity to surprise the Irish settled in Brega and, in a dawn attack, killed their king and gained a complete victory over them. He took much plunder and slaves from whom he learned of the wealth amassed by the Norse in Dublin. Ragnar sailed into Dublin bay to survey the fortifications and lie of the land but knew he was too weak to attempt any venture here and went on down the east coast to the south of Ireland. Here they explored the Norse fortification at Waterford which, though well protected from the land, was vulnerable from the sea and Ragnar decided to attack it. The fortification comprised a wooden palisade fronted by a ditch, but the seaward side had minimal defences, with a marshy bog at the foreshore and a narrow stone causeway giving access to their ships.

The leader of the Norse at Waterford was Marsteinn, who had time to organise those men in the fortification and its shore defences. Ragnar with full thrust beached his ships into the black bog, and the warriors leapt into the rotting morass, some sinking up to their chests and struggling to move forward. Ragnar had arranged for his bowmen to release a shower of arrows to hold back the defenders during this vulnerable period, but soon his men were on dry land and making good effect of themselves. The defenders fought hard, but were soon overwhelmed by Ragnar's men and Marsteinn was killed. The fortification was sacked and Ragnar was astounded by the amount of wealth, much of it gold, which they recovered. Gunnr and Finn had used their bows to good effect from the ships, but had not yet experienced fighting man to man. They were eager to get ashore for plunder and both Gunnr and Finn were able to obtain spears and axes which they prized greatly.

Knowing they would be unable to hold the fortification, once the Norse had organised resistance from the outside, Ragnar put to sea and sailed to some small islands close by to the east. There they camped and Ragnar conferred with his sons and with Bullr.

Ragnar said, "We have now been well rewarded for our efforts and learnt enough of this country to better plan the taking of its great promise. I suggest we share our rewards now and return home for I intend to raise a fleet sufficient to take Dublin and become the over-lord of these provinces." The next day the fleet sailed south, and then along the southern belly of England to reach the North Sea and to follow the sea-lane up the Friesian coast.

Once home on Zealand, there was much joy at the reunion with Aslaug and her daughters who came down to meet the ships but it was tinged with sadness on hearing of the loss of Rognvald and Hvitserkr. There was great interest as the plunder was unloaded, shared and taken away for safe storage. Once unloaded, the ships masts and rigging were lowered and taken ashore, and the ships then hauled on land for the winter. In the warmth of the hall, the events of the expedition were related and the happenings on Zealand discussed, animated by the flow of beer and good food.

The winter brought particularly harsh weather with heavy snows persisting well into the following year and drifting on to icy ground.

Ragnar and his sons had plenty of time to plan their attack on Dublin and to organise the necessary work once the snow had gone. Ragnar's relationship with Aslaug improved and some genuine warmth was exchanged between them. Once the ground had cleared, Ragnar began building ships to replace those lost and damaged. The large oak trees were felled and cut to provide the keels and the planking. The green timbers comprising the planking were bent into place and secured to the keel and one to the other with iron rivets. The ribs were lashed in place with pine roots, and the oak keelson lain down to step the pine mast. The planking was caulked with wool and pine tar and the steering board oar attached by a withy of pine root. Because of the late start to the summer and the work required on the ships being built, Ragnar decided to spend the summer dealing with matters on Zealand, not least because a civil war had broken out among the Danish Royal family and he feared it might spill over into his territory. On mid-summer's day they had a break from their work to celebrate and enjoy the ensuing festivities with the lighting of the Bale-Fire. By late autumn, the fleet was complete in all respects and was then laid up ready for the expedition in the following spring. That winter was the last that Ragnar and his sons would spend together.

The following spring the crews came together and the ships were launched. The two friends, Gunnr and Finn were among the crews as experienced veterans. They had filled out into strong young men. They had secured places in a ship under one of the Jarls, and were now well fitted out with weapons. The provisions were put on board comprising dried fish, mainly cod gutted and hung over wooden poles to be dried by the sea air and sun. The fish was lightweight but very hard needing to be cut with a serrated edged knife and eaten cold. They also loaded dried and salted meat, dried berries, oats and water, and the crews took on board their sea chests and weapons. Excitement grew as the ships pulled out into the Sound, a mighty fleet of capable men with a sense of invincibility against all the fates.

Aslaug cried, foreseeing in a premonition that she would not see any of her sons or husband again. The ships had a good passage sailing to the north of Denmark and out into the North Sea where they made there way south and along the shallow coastal waters of Friesland with its many shoals and sand banks. They entered the English Channel and then out into the Atlantic Ocean, before turning north towards the Irish Sea. They eventually arrived off Dublin Bay in the early summer of the year 851AD.

The sky and sea had merged in a light grey mist and the Norse Sea Ward was the first to see the Danish sails, which appeared as though they were suspended in the air with sea and sky blending into one. The Norse correctly surmised that it was a Danish fleet coming to plunder Dublin and a panic set in. They sent out a fast ship to meet the approaching fleet and to ascertain its intent, which continued to grow in size as more ships came over the horizon.

As the Norse ship drew near the leading ship of the fleet, the helmsman called out, "You, men, from what country do you come upon the sea. Do you come for peace or war?"

The leading ship replied with a storm of arrows, and soon the ships were engaged and the Norse crew were slain. Ragnar directed his fleet to where the Norse ships lay at anchor, and running his ships in towards the shore, they were met by the Norse defenders. The battle was very fierce. For every man he lost, three times that number of Norse was killed. The heads of all the wounded were cut off and, having overcome the defences, they marched on the fort and took all the women, gold and possessions of the Norsemen that they had stolen from the churches and the men of Erin and they took them aboard their ships.

Gunnr and Finn had been at the forefront of the assault, working together both in attack and defence alongside their Jarl. Neither had received any injuries. They spoke animatedly after the battle about their experiences, suddenly tired as their battle juices drained away, relieved to be alive and to have won the day. This was the first time they had fought man to man. They had benefited greatly from the skill of their fellow Danes fighting alongside them. Both collected fine swords from the fallen enemy. Finn composed a drapa – a short poem, to record the day.

> The hot blood rises high
> The brain races with fear and excitement
> The battle cry wells from deep below
> But I hear nothing, so fixed is my mind
> As the linden shields and swords clash
> And the earth is reddened with blood
> My courage, my will, and my stamina
> Comes to me from my father's line
> I am sorely tried, but he has not failed me.

Ragnar decided to sail his ships north and to anchor in Carlingford Lough where he could better protect his fleet. From here he attacked the Norse stronghold of Annagassan, a short distance south of Carlingford Lough across a bay. Having taken Annagassan, he subdued the area round about and received their submission.

Ragnar made Ivarr king of Dublin. He strengthened the defences and housed his own men. As was the way of Ivarr, he sought an ally against the Norse settlers who, he knew, would seek revenge. He made representations to the Irish King Cerball of Ossary who had suffered at the hands of the Norse and who had been instrumental in the death of Thorgisl and they entered into an alliance. Meanwhile, Ragnar had settled his men around Carlingford Lough near to his ships for the coming winter.

Two of the Norse Jarls, Steinn and Jargna had gone far and wide to raise an army to win back their losses. By the spring of 852AD, they had raised a fleet of 160 ships, far outnumbering Ragnar's Danish fleet, which they attacked with fury. They fought for two days in the loch and the losses were great on both sides. By the second day Ragnar's men were facing defeat and becoming dispirited with the odds stacked against them. They had been cut off from their provisions, and were weakened by the fighting and lack of food.

In the evening, as the fighting died down, Ragnar addressed his men to rally them, "We are sorely tried and outnumbered, but the victory will be all the sweeter when it comes. I have not brought you across the seas to see the gains we have made now slip away. Tomorrow those who are not chosen by the Valkyries to go to the hall of Odin and to fight his final battle, they will prevail with me. We may go hungry tonight, but the wind favours our position and it is the hungriest dog that wins the fight. Let us therefore sail at first light whilst the enemy sleeps off its excesses of the night, and let us ram their ships, and see our berserkers on their decks before their legs can recover themselves. For tonight let our bodies be well fed with a deep and refreshing sleep, and when we awake in the cold morning light, with hunger gnawing at our bellies, we shall be driven to win this fight."

Ragnar's men were uplifted by his address, and so it came to pass. At first light, Ragnar's ships were on the water and amongst the Norse ships, each of his men becoming a berserker, fearless in their fury. Once the Norse began to break, Jarl Steinn fled ashore and escaped, but Jarl Jargna was captured and beheaded.

With the Norse settlers thus spent, Ivarr, as was his way, became restless for action. He was never content to sit on his gains but always hungered for a new challenge to his physical and mental abilities. He decided that he would re-enforce Dublin's over-lordship on the Vikings based on the island of Noirmoutier on the west coast of France, and to explore the links established with the Arabs in Spain. Ragnar was strongly opposed to this, arguing that they needed to consolidate the hold on their gains, but he could do little to stop him taking his ships and men to France. Sigurdr was left in charge of Dublin, whilst the other brothers, Ubbe, Halfdan and Bjorn sailed with Ivarr as did the Jarl's ship on which Gunnr and Finn sailed.

Ragnar missed the support of his sons, but carried on establishing himself in his newly acquired province, enforcing his mastery in all the regions. The displaced leader of the Norse in Dublin, a hard and bitter man called Helr whose name meant a rock, planned to capture and kill Ragnar in revenge, studying his movements and habits. He noted that he would often go to check on the safety of his ships laid to in the loch, arriving an hour before nightfall, and then checking on the alertness of his guards. He usually went with a light force on horseback. Helr, with a band of men, hid themselves waiting to waylay Ragnar. It was many nights before the chance arose, when Ragnar and his companions were surrounded and attacked. Ragnar was pulled from his horse, overpowered and bound, and then taken to a house where Helr began to torture him. He was burnt, cut and speared in his limbs.

Ragnar called out, "What coward is this that needs to provoke a man tied up so that he cannot move?"

"Silence you Danish pig," said Helr, "You took my daughter in Dublin, and she is now a Danish slave."

Ragnar replied, "If the young pigs knew how the old boar suffers, they would scream loudly."

"I don't fear your threats," said Helr, "The kings of Vestfold will take back their possessions before your pigs come out of the forest." Helr continued to torture Ragnar, but Ragnar gave him little satisfaction, conceding nothing. Helr, recognising a brave man then, tired of his game, cut off his head with his axe. Ragnar was then thrown into a rubbish pit. He died at the age of 53 as he had lived, resolute in the face of adversity and accepting his inevitable fate with courage.

Sigurdr, on hearing of his father's capture became incensed, and began to interrogate the Norse in a wild and threatening manner and, fearing for their lives, they gave up Helr's place of safety. Sigurdr found and killed him, but Ragnar's body was never found. Such a king, so distinguished in battle, was thus denied the Viking burial that he deserved.

Two months later a large fleet arrived off Dublin, led by Olafr hviti - Olafr the White, a son of the king of Vestfold, who history records as Olafr Geirstadaalfr, a tall man and a true warrior king. Sigurdr, without the support of his brothers and their forces and with the death of Ragnar, was forced to submit the Danes to Olafr's rule as the new king of Dublin. Olafr was quick to strengthen and renew the alliance with King Cerball of Ossory recognising its strategic importance.

Olafr was no stranger to the waters around Pictland and Ireland. He had established his rights as overlord of the Orkneys, the Hebrides and the Norse settlers in Ireland. Indeed he had married the daughter of Ketill flatnefr - Ketill Flat Nose. Ketill and his kinsmen had been driven off their lands in Norway by an avaricious king and had then become freebooters around the area. Eventually he and his kinsmen had brought the Hebrides under his control, where he settled with his wife Yngvild. He had two sons, Bjorn the Easterner and Helgi Bjolan, and also three daughters, Jorunn the wise, Thorunn and Audr djupaudga - Aud the Deep Minded. Before leaving Norway, Thorunn was married to Helgi the Lean, and the couple then sailed with Thorunn's brothers, Bjorn and Helgi Bjolan to Iceland where they founded large settlements.

Olafr had stayed at Ketill Flat Nose's long house whilst establishing his control over the area. The long house comprised stonewalls bulging outwards at the middle of the longer walls, but upright at the end walls. Inside the walls was a timber cladding held in place with wooden uprights. The rafters were seated on the wooden uprights, and the roof above the rafters was sealed with more timber cladding. On the timber roof, sods of turf were laid, held down by ropes weighted with stones. The central room had benches around it for sleeping partitioned as necessary, and a hearth for the fire was central to the room, with smoke finding its way through a hole in the roof. The area at one end was where the livestock would be kept in winter, and at the other end was an area for storage. There was little space for a large family. Guests had to fit in where they could.

Olafr was attracted to Aud's intelligent and lively personality whilst discussing matters with Ketill Flat Nose in the long house, which led to their romance. On marrying Aud, he established a base in the Hebrides and, in between his expeditions, he fathered a son called Thorsteinn raudr - Thorsteinn the Red. In later years, his son married Thuridr the grand daughter of King Cerball of Ossory, and with the Jarls of Orkney he created a kingdom in Pictland embracing Sutherland, Caithness, Moray and Ross. Aud for her part eventually went to Iceland to join her brothers and sister, and was the subject of the Icelandic Laxardal saga detailing the establishment of her settlement there.

Olafr, hearing of the Danes' success, had raised a fleet to reclaim his rights over the Norse settlers. On his way he had stopped off in the Hebrides to see Aud, to learn what he could of the events in Ireland and to establish a tributary from the Hebrides. The latter objective led to a major rift between Ketill Flat Nose and Olafr. Ketill had exploded in fury against his son in law and Olafr left making threats that he would return to collect his due if necessary by force. Ketill who had risked much to make the Hebrides a Norse colony did not take kindly to such threats and trouble was bound to follow.

Ivarr was unaware of events in Dublin following his departure on a voyage that had been very stormy with lightning and thunder, and at several times he had felt it necessary to make sacrifices to Thor, the god of thunder, as the spume whipped up the back of the waves. Some men thought they were in the sea of Elivagar - the venom cold waves of a calamitous sea. The weather eased but left a heavy swell rolling in from the southwest. Eventually they reached the island of Noirmoutier at the mouth of the River Loire, sailing around to the lee side and anchoring close inshore.

The Norse Vikings came out ready to fight, unsure of Ivarr's intentions. Ivarr sent a boat ashore with a messenger, to advise them that Ivarr the Boneless, the king of Dublin, had come to visit his tributary and to receive their hospitality. Asgeir, their leader, was cautious but knew of Ivarr's reputation, and sent back his greetings and welcome. Ivarr brought his men ashore, and that night Asgeir prepared a feast, roasting sheep and providing copious drinks of wine. Ivarr and Asgeir got on very well, and Ivarr was very interested to hear of their expedition up the River Loire, and the sacking of Nantes less than a days sail up the river and, in particular, to know of the weakness of Charles the Bald. Asgeir related how Charles, faced with a revolt in Brittany, and having led his forces against them, had in the heat of battle deserted his forces. When the cry went up, "Where is the king," panic had set in followed by defeat. He also related how Godfred commanding the Vikings in the Seine country, under the leadership of Sidroc, had faced down Charles and his older brother Lothair. The two brothers had met to form a joint attack on the Vikings at their camp at Givold's grave but in the final events, Charles paid a large amount in gold and silver for the Vikings to leave, not fully trusting his brother, nor his own abilities. Ivarr enquired about the River Loire and its navigability, to which Asgeir confirmed that the river was navigable at least a hundred miles above the city of Nantes which they had previously sacked, and with their combined fleets they could penetrate further upstream and overwhelm any resistance without fear of being cut off.

Ivarr and Asgeir agreed they would go up the River Loire to attack deep in the heart of France. The combined large fleet rowed its way up the river past Nantes, a formidable sight to those on the banks and a sight of terror to those settlements where the fleet anchored and the men came ashore to cook the animals taken in passing, and to have sport with the local inhabitants. Having travelled over 100 miles past Nantes which they had again attacked. They came to the city of Tours, and saw the abbeys of St. Martin of Tours one inside the city walls and the older one outside the walls at Marmoutiers. The ships anchored in the river, covering it to such an extent that it looked like a solid mass of wood and the Vikings immediately stormed ashore, stepping from ship to ship. They first attacked the abbey at Marmoutier before storming the city walls, and going on to sack the abbey and town with little resistance and amongst wide spread panic. The fleet acquired a great deal of plunder and arrived back at Noirmoutier with little loss.

Ivarr's taste was whetted for the continent's potential for gain and easy access through its long rivers, and Asgeir told him of a river called the Adour in Gascony near the border with Spain, which rose in the Pyrenees and was navigable over much of its length but had not been explored. Once rested, they decided to see what the river might hold and were able to penetrate as far as Tarbes, 120 miles from the river's mouth. Their raids were successful but, on their return, they lost men in numerous battles with the Basques they called the mountaineers, and the prizes were hard won against opponents with an insatiable desire to fight, just as they had done against Charles the Great's army returning from Spain.

Gunnr and Finn had been fascinated to see these new balmy lands, with their stone buildings and foreign people and language. They had lived well on the freshly cooked sheep and cattle they had captured and roasted on the riverbanks and they had tasted grapes and wine for the first time in their lives and eventually oranges. Not all had been pleasant. The mosquitoes had bothered them and their encounter with the Basque mountaineers had been a dramatic experience for them. They felt lucky to have survived, for the Basques had been relentless in their wish to attack them. Ivarr had been convinced that he should avoid them in future.

Bjorn woke one night from an overpowering and vivid dream, leaving him very shaken. He dreamt that his father was alone and facing death in extreme circumstances and that his brother Sigurdr was also in dire danger. He pleaded with Ivarr to return to Dublin, but Ivarr ever eager to press on and discover new situations was determined to know more about the Arabs and Spain. He fought many battles with the Arabs, choosing not to ally or negotiate for the trading slaves but set his heart on conquest. They sailed on to Lisbon, which they began to siege but they were unable to break through its walls and abandoned the siege.

On leaving Lisbon and sailing out of the long bay at the mouth of the River Tagus, the fleet was intercepted by Arab ships built in the form of galleys rowed by slaves. The Arab ships were more stable in the water as fighting platforms and were heavily built and capable of ramming other ships. Two long ships had been attacked in this way and disabled and the long ship on which Finn and Gunnr sailed was targeted by an Arab ship, that rowed at pace towards them. Those on board were unsure how to react to this threat but prepared themselves for defence. As the Arab ship bore down on the long ship's port quarter, Finn, braving the missiles from the platform decks on the Arab ship, picked up the aftermost heavy wooden tee piece, one of three wooden upright posts on which the oars and other items could be stowed when not in use. Lifting it high above his head, Finn threw it at the prow of the Arab ship just before impact. In consequence the planking was not stove in, but the wooden post took the brunt of the impact, causing the stern to be pushed around, leaving the two ships lying port side to port side. This severely hampered the rowers on the port side of the Arab ship, and many of them lost their oars under the hull of the long ship. The position of the long ship also exposed them to view through a gap in the superstructure. The new situation that had developed was quickly taken advantage of by the Vikings as they rained down their arrows and spears on to the rowers. The Arab ship's ability to move was temporally stopped dead as confusion reigned, and Gunnr seized the sheets of the sail to take advantage of a cross wind, and so the long ship was moved out to sea and escaped. The crew were full of praise for Finn's quick thinking and the perfect timing of his action. They lauded the strength he had shown in lifting up the wooden post, recognising that he had saved the ship from certain capture and their lives from death or enslavement.

They carried on south towards the entrance to the Mediterranean known as the Pillars of Hercules, (Straits of Gibraltar) and sighting Cadiz, decided to attack the city. Here they had more success and were able to breach the walls and to plunder the city at will. Encouraged by this, they entered the River Guadalquivir just to the north, rowing up a lazy river banked by orange groves and on to Seville, which they attacked. They captured and plundered the suburbs with ease but could not take the city and lost many men in the process before abandoning the action.

By this time, Ivarr had been away from Dublin for over two years and they decided to sail the fleet back to Noirmoutier where Ivarr learnt of the death of Ragnar, and the transfer of power in Dublin to Olafr the White. Asgeir had become a close comrade of Ivarr, respecting his judgement, and he was sorry to hear of Ragnar's misfortune. Ivarr knew Olafr of old and after careful thought decided not to take any precipitate action against such a strong king. He had heard of successful raids by other Viking bands in England and decided to join them. .

A Danish leader called Hastein, who had established a camp on the island of Thanet at the southern side of the mouth of the River Thames was joined by Ivarr. Ivarr had the larger forces and so established himself as their leader. The Isle of Thanet was a large island off the eastern coast of Kent, separated by a wide tidal seaway known as the Wantsum Channel through which ships could pass into the Thames. It was sheltered and ideal for laying up the longships and a natural defence against attacks from Kent with only two fords at low tide.

Ivarr learnt of Hastein's previous exploits with the leader Rorik. Rorik was based in Frisia having won large tracts of land there from King Lothair, assisted by King Godfred. In 851AD when, as part of a fleet of three hundred and fifty ships led by Rorik, they had sailed to England and stormed and sacked Canterbury by sailing up the River Stour. On returning they sailed back through the Wantsum Channel into the River Thames and on to London where they had killed Brihtwulf, the king of Mercia and put his forces to flight.

However their confidence over reached them when they crossed over the River Thames into Surrey and were met by King Aethelwulf of Wessex and his elder son Aethelbold at Aclea (Okley). Here the Danes were routed and the English described it as the greatest slaughter of the heathens. Ivarr had developed a healthy respect for the kingdom of Wessex which had shown more steel than the men of Mercia.

They get smart blows instead of shillings
And the hammer's weight instead of rings

Ivarr set about improving the defences on Thanet, a task to which the Danes proved extremely adept. Should the camp's outer defences be breached, they had devised killing zones and areas of ambush that were not detectable to any attacker. Ivarr's caution was well justified for Ealdormen Huda and Ealhere had raised the Fyrd of Kent and Surrey and came to attack with determination and courage. Many were slain on both sides but repeated charges by the English failed to dislodge the Danes and so they withdrew.

This was the first time that Gunnr and Finn had come across the Anglo Saxons, whose language they could understand and who seemed very similar to their own people. Gunnr and Finn learnt a great deal about the art of fortification, the use of natural defensive features and the deployment of defensive forces to maximise their effectiveness.

At this time, Ivarr learnt that there was rebellion brewing in the house of Wessex. King Aethelwulf, on the death of his wife Osburgh, had travelled to see the Pope, staying at the court of Charles the Bald on the way to Rome. Charles had introduced his young daughter to the elderly king, with a view to some form of joint alliance against the Viking bands. On his return King Aethelwulf decided to marry Charles the Bald's daughter Judith, then aged twelve years old. He stayed at the court a long time, and his elder son Aethelbald considered he was neglecting the kingdom especially with a Viking army wintering nearby for the first time. He also heard that, contrary to Saxon custom, Charles the Bald had insisted that Judith should sit alongside King Aethelwulf and be named as Queen. With the support of Ealhstan, the Bishop of Sherbourne, and Eanwulf the Ealdorman of Somerset, Aethelbald took over the kingdom. On Aethelwulf's return, the kingdom had divided loyalties and a civil war was threatening. However, a compromise was reached, whereby Aethebald took over the western and stronger half of the kingdom and Aethelwulf took over the smaller eastern half incorporating Kent.

Bjorn had formed a strong friendship with Hastein, and was excited by the tales of his expeditions in northern France. His interest in the kingdom had been kindled by his expeditions with Ivarr. They agreed to form an alliance to make further attacks on the country and Bjorn advised Ivarr of his intention to take his ships out of the fleet. "We have journeyed and prospered well together but I now wish to make my own destiny and win glory by my own merit. Dublin holds few prospects for me, a bitter fight with the Norse, or a watering down of command." Ivarr was sorry to lose the support of one of his able brothers but accepted his right to take his own decisions. Bjorn sailed with Hastein in 854AD.

Ivarr now considered his position on Thanet with a reduced force and was aware that the great forest known as the Andredsweald provided a formidable barrier to raids further west. He decided to move his forces to a larger island, the Isle of Sheppey, situated further up the River Thames towards London, enabling raids into northern Kent to take a shorter and more direct route, which he now considered to be more vulnerable to Viking attack. During this time, Ivarr learnt much about the different English kingdoms, their strengths and weaknesses and their methods of defence and attack. Ivarr came to the conclusion that he needed an ally and greater strength, and in particular, Ragnar's fleet under the control of Sigurdr. Moreover, knowing Olafr the White, he thought there would be a chance to negotiate an alliance between them and so he decided to return to Dublin.

In the year 856AD, Ivarr returned to the waters off Dublin and met Ragnar's fleet commanded by Sigurdr who were returning from an attack on Anglesey, - the island of the moon renamed by King Edwin of Northumbria on its conquest two hundred years before. Sigurdr and Ivarr greeted one another with great warmth. Ivarr was keen to know more of the death of Ragnar and the kingship of Olaf, whilst Sigurdr wished to know of Ivarr's expeditions. The two talked for many hours with the fleets drifting in the sea. The combined fleets then sailed in to land, anchoring off Dublin. Ivarr sent a message of greetings to Olafr, stating he had come in peace to discuss an alliance. Olafr equally did not want to fight the Danes with their strong fleet and reputation and with Ivarr having already been established as the king of Dublin and the Norse settlements. He was also being hard pressed by the High King Malachy, who had formed an alliance with the Gaill Gaedhil, some Norse settlers and a mixture of Norse Gaelic stock, living in the Hebrides and across the water in Pictland. These forces were led by none other than Ketill Flat Nose seeking the expulsion of Olafr from Ireland.

Ivarr and Olafr agreed to meet on neutral territory on board one of the ships, with just three retainers in attendance to each of the leaders. They welcomed one another and seated themselves on the sea chests.

Ivarr began, "I see no point in a quarrel between the Norse and the Danes over parcels of land when together we have all the kingdoms in England and Pictland for the taking. We know one another of old and so I propose a joint alliance between us. We shall be joint kings of Dublin, and protect one another's interests and, where we fight together, we will share our gains equally."

"What you say makes much sense," said Olafr, "for I recognise that you and your brothers make a powerful ally which will enhance both our prospects and I know of your reputation to bring success with you."

The alliance was therefore agreed between them and the fleet moved into the harbour and beached their ships where they could, setting up their tents ashore. The order was given by Olafr that freshly killed sheep should be supplied to the Danish crews, who then started their campfires, roasting the sheep on a spit and baking bread on a flat stone by the fire. They began to celebrate the alliance with ale and fresh food, welcome after the dried food consumed on their sea voyage and the staple food of porridge made from grass seeds such as goosefoot and knotgrass.

Ivarr and his brothers Sigurdr and Halfdan along with the Jarls were given comfortable accommodation in Dublin and a feast was held that night to cement the agreement and to plan the future course of their exploits. All in Dublin were in a high state of merriment and after the last five years of heavy campaigning since leaving Zealand, Ivarr in a rare moment relaxed his focused mind and went with the mood of the night, after making a sacrifice to Odin and Frey to ensure the alliance would prove beneficial to him. Olafr warmed to a light hearted Ivarr and the laughter generated was infectious and brought the two leaders close together. The alliance coincided with the Vinternatsblot festival, the welcome to winter festival of October 14th, to which the Vikings had been looking forward and had already prepared.

As the festivities moved on into the night, Ivarr started a conversation with Thora, the daughter of a Norse Jarl. She was much shorter than Ivarr, being only five feet six inches in height. She had a short upturned nose, a wide mouth with full lips, and large blue intelligent eyes in a round and interesting face. She was pretty but not beautiful. It was however her intellect that caught Ivarr's interest. They began to discuss matters in great depth. Ivarr had never met a woman who he had found both intellectually challenging and stimulating and, after five years seafaring, his senses were heightened to Thora's attractions. They carried on talking until the dawn was breaking, covering all manner of topics including Ivarr's religion and his knowledge of the Irish, the English, the Franks and the Arabs in Spain, subjects which interested Thora greatly. They reluctantly parted company but the next night Ivarr called in to see the Jarl and to renew his acquaintance with Thora. Ivarr's thoughts no longer focused on the next campaign. He was into a totally new thought pattern centred on Thora. Over the next few weeks the relationship developed to the point where Ivarr asked the Jarl for permission to marry his daughter. The marriage was agreed, the financial arrangements were made between the parties, and the marriage of the joint kings of Dublin took place in a style befitting the importance of the occasion.

The alliance made and cemented on that historic day between the Norse and the Danes led to the conquest of England and to the establishment of the Danelaw and, in due course, to the establishment of a single kingdom called Scotland.

Chapter 5

OLAFR AND IVARR

Olafr and Ivarr had known each other in their younger days and were already good friends. They developed a mutual respect in their maturity. Both were very tall, powerfully built, capable men, and had the presence and manner of natural leaders. Olafr had rugged good looks with a strong jutting chin and a straight nose with little apparent bridge to the nose and a reddish beard. His body was round and straight with long legs. Ivarr's features on the other hand were more regular, with thinking eyes that portrayed a shrewd intelligence. His body was impressive, with a long broad and angular back, muscular and supported by a narrow waist and thickset legs, which were short in comparison to his back. It was his movements that portrayed his intimidating strength, fast in his reactions and supple like a coiled snake, able to strike unexpectedly in any direction. As he walked, he gave the impression of being ready for action, an intimidating stance hard to define.

The two leaders were quick to bring each other up to date with their latest news. Whilst food was being prepared on an open fire they began to formulate their future plans.

"What news of Vestfold," asked Ivarr, "for I have been away for many years now. How is your father King Godfrith?"

"Not good news," said Olafr, "my mother died, and as you will know, when she married my father she was princess Alfhildr and so brought with her half of the kingdom of Vingulmork. His right to retain it on her death caused problems with Vingulmork, of which the Grenlanders and King Haraldr inn granraudi of Agdir took full advantage. In settling his rights, my father killed King Haraldr but, with my mother gone, he made the foolish decision to forcibly marry

King Agdir's daughter, Asa. They had a son who they called Halfdan svarti – Halfdan the Black, and black was that day for my father was assassinated when the boy was only one year old. I suspect Asa had a hand in his death. She remains at his hall and I can foresee future trouble now that I am King of Vestfold."

"Such news is not good," said Ivarr, "but the boy is still young and will pose no threat for many years. I have heard little of how matters lie in Zealand and Viken since my father's death. We have the strength of many brothers and for this I do not fear any challenges."

Ivarr asked how the situation in Ireland had developed since his departure.

Olafr replied, "Soon after I arrived in Dublin, the High King Malachy of the southern O'Neil asserted control over the kings of Munster, taking their fortress at Cashel. Since then he has allied with Ketill Flat Nose, the Hofthingi of the Hebrides, who, besides being their chieftain, also leads many of the Gaill Gaedhil on the mainland. They pose a real and growing threat. Ketill is my father in law and we are on bad terms. I suspect he wants to avoid paying tribute due to Vestfold, and so wishes to aid my defeat in this region."

"What allies do we have", asked Ivarr, "and who might we bring to our side?"

"We have maintained the alliance you formed with King Cerball of Ossory before you left Dublin. Though he had suffered at our hands, I recognised his value as an ally against our Irish enemies and we made peace", said Olafr.

"But what of the kingdom of Ciannachta, near the Norse settlements at Anagassan?" asked Ivarr. "In the year I became king of Dublin, Malachy had captured Cinaed, son of King Conaing, and had drowned him in a sack in the Nanny River because he had allied with the Norse."

Olafr replied "His brother King Flann seeks revenge against Malachy for putting Cinaed to such a dishonourable death. King Flann has therefore also formed an alliance with us to this end, but his forces are not large. A greater prize would be an alliance with his uncle, King Aed Findliath of the northern O'Neil, who is ambitious and wants to be the next High King. Malachy has plundered his territory this year, and ambition is now richly flavoured with hatred for the death of his nephew and the wanton wasting of his kingdom."

"Then let us work on Flann to bring about such an alliance", said Ivarr, "and in the meantime let us meet Ketill Flat Nose in the field whilst he operates alone and before he has had time to combine his forces with those of Malachy." Ivarr continued, "As you know we Danes took your stronghold at Vedrafjordr (Waterford) and defeated Marsteinn their leader. Seeing this fortification as being vulnerable to attack from the sea, our Jarl Rodolf has established a much stronger seaward fortification on the borders of Ossory, at the top of the Vedrafjordr. The spit of land between the meeting of the Rivers Barrow and Glasha has been enclosed with a twelve-foot palisade, and a water ditch outside has been dug from the river Glasha to the river Barrow, beside which is marshland. In consequence, the defences of the fortification is bound by the river Glasha on one side, a ditch and marsh on the other side, and on the south is an entrance into the fortification from the river Barrow through which we can take our ships. We can take as many as 30 ships inside the fortification which has many longhouses and space for tents to accommodate a thousand men and it also has an inner fortification. This fortification would be very difficult to attack. We can use it as a base to support King Cerball of Ossory and to campaign into neighbouring Munster".

And so it was agreed. Ivarr and Olafr campaigned against the forces of Ketill Flat Nose operating in Munster against their King Maelguala. A series of skirmishes took place at which Ketill Flat Nose was routed. In the following year, Ketill Flat Nose having strengthened his forces, led a more serious encounter that took place at Arra in northwest Munster when King Cerball of Ossory gave support to the Vikings. The forces of Ketill Flat Nose were crushed and, from this time on, they ceased to be a factor in the affairs of Ireland. Ketill escaped and returned to the Hebrides.

Meanwhile, King Malachy had undertaken a third expedition into Munster to assert his control, and the Kings of Munster were defeated. Malachy took hostages from as far afield as the Leinster borders up to Cork. Ivarr, hearing of this campaign, invaded Malachy's territory of Mide as a reprisal. He was unopposed and carried off much valuable plunder.

In the following year of 859, Malachy sought to bring peace and agreement among the Irish. He summoned all the kings of Erin to a Royal Assembly at the church of Rath Aeda. This was situated near a fortress among the Midland lakes. When those attending had gathered together, the meeting was presided over by the abbots of Armagh and Clonard.

The Abbot of Armagh began, "It is with much regret that I do not see the face of Aed Findliath among you, the King of the northern O'Neils. Nor do I see King Flann of Ciannachta. We sons of Erin have spilt much blood between us for motives that are rarely honourable, and in doing so we have opened up our wounds for the Danes and the Lochlainn to bleed us further. We could yet bleed to death, unless you royal kings can unite under the leadership of your High King Malachy who has been tireless in his pursuit of the Heathen. I ask you to swear allegiance to your lord on the holy relics in the presence of your abbots."

The defeated King of Munster, Maelguala, was the first to swear his allegiance but it did him little good, for Ivarr captured him later that year and killed him for allying with Malachy. Cerball of Ossory was reluctant to swear his allegiance and had contemplated attacking Malachy with the help of the Danes when Malachy had invaded Munster to force the submission of King Maelguala. The abbots threatened Cerball with damnation and excommunication and Malachy put him under extreme pressure, not least since he was married to Malachy's daughter by an earlier marriage and Malachy was married to Lann, the sister of Cerball. He reluctantly capitulated to their demands but behind the mask he did not submit. Malachy then committed all his under-kings to support him on a military campaign to invade the territory of King Aed Findliath and to cause his death or submission.

When Ivarr and Olafr heard about the Royal Assembly from King Flann and the intended invasion, a meeting was quickly arranged with Flann's uncle Aed Findliath. Before the meeting, a minor Norse leader, living south of the Scottish kingdom and on the west coast, came to see Ivarr and Olafr. His name was Auisle, a stockily built man, five foot nine inches tall, having a round head with a down-turned mouth. He was cock sure of himself, talking above his station and never missed a chance to enhance himself. Ivarr disliked him, suspecting that he had been involved with Ketill Flat Nose and now, seeing a change in the wind, decided to switch his allegiance to better prospects. Olafr was more interested in his connections and stories of great potential in the land of the Picts knowing of the success of his son Thorsteinn the Red in gaining territory in the north of the Pictish kingdom. Auisle claimed to have met King Cinaed MacAlpin and his sons Constantine and Aed of the small Scottish kingdom of Dal Riada, confined to the Western Isles and the land north of the lower reaches of the River Clyde. The Dal Riada kingdom bordered Pictland to the north and east, whilst to the south, the British Kingdom of Strathclyde stretched from England up to the banks of the River Clyde. Auisle maintained that King Cinaed MacAlpin was greedy to extend his kingdom into Pictland and Strathclyde but lacked the forces to hold territory. To the east of the Strathclyde kingdom was the English kingdom of North Humberland which Auisle claimed was unsettled with rival claims to the kingdom and in a state of civil war. Ivarr was interested in the latter claim and sent spies into North Humberland to learn more of the kingdom. Auisle was thus taken into the alliance because of his apparent knowledge.

Ivarr and Olafr joined up with King Flann and the party went to meet King Aed Findliath. On reaching the hall, King Flann went forward to greet his uncle, embracing him warmly. Behind him strode Olaff, Ivarr and his brother Sigurdr, three physically impressive leaders, so different to the portly priests and retainers around King Aed Finliath. Aed was relatively short, but he was thick set and muscular and a man of determined character and presence. After Flann's introduction, Olafr presented King Aed Findliath with a well-crafted and decorative sword.

Once seated in the hall, Olafr came straight to the point saying, "The Norse and Danish Kings of Dublin come in peace, and seek an alliance with you to strengthen both parties and further our joint interests. We know of the recent meeting of the Royal Assembly called by King Malachy which has strengthened his forces and we also know that he wishes neither of us any good".

Aed Finliath knew much more and was aware that Malachy was already preparing to invade his territory. This was inevitable once he had the allegiance of the other kings. He could not therefore ignore the insult that Aed Findliath's absence had caused. Aed Finliath also recognised the power created by the alliance of the Norse and Danes and knew they were also a real threat outside an alliance with him.

"Your offer is most welcome", said Aed "and your alliance with Flann has been a good example of the benefits of your co-operation. Let us, therefore, join together against Malachy and his under-kings, and meet them in the field once they are in our territory. I would first want to talk with him and know his demands, when faced with our strength."

"That is wise", said Ivarr, "A little knowledge can be worth many warriors. I will send a man to bring all our forces here."

"Then let us drink, dance and feast tonight to celebrate and strengthen our ties", said Aed Finliath.

Aed proved a good host. As the evening wore on, all were in a high state of merriment. Recognising that the Norse had the greater number of men settled in Ireland, he sought out Olafr to find out more about his background. Olafr told him that he was the King of Vestfold, the Orkneys and the Hebrides and joint King of Dublin. Aed asked him if he was married.

Olafr replied, "I was married to Aud, the daughter of Ketill Flat Nose, who you know as Ketill Find – the Fair. As you will know, he was an ally of Malachy and we have defeated him in several battles, so that his men are no longer a force in Ireland. I have a son called Thorsteinn by Aud, but the last time I saw her, we were estranged and her father openly defied me."

Aed replied, "I have many daughters and it would please me to seal our pact in a blood- relationship. Should it be to your liking, I would offer my daughter Lann to be your wife. I will send for her to meet you."

Olafr was indeed taken by her good looks with her thick black hair and eyes and her womanly figure. They warmed to one another and

83

Olafr later told Aed he would be honoured to marry Lann. It was then arranged for the couple to marry the next day and the celebrations carried through until daybreak.

The marriage was to be a Christian ceremony and the priests came out in their resplendent robes to officiate. Lann, bedecked in flowers, was dressed in white and accompanied by her sisters. Olafr understood nothing of the ceremony, which seemed to go on forever. He was told what to say at the appropriate moment.

After the ceremony, the musicians began to play, and the dancing began with wild abandon. Everyone suddenly became revived from the nights' excesses, and the celebrations took off anew.

Aed made a speech praising his daughter and said, "I drink to this union and may the first child be a boy, the first Mac Lochlainn", for they referred to the Norse as the men of the lakes. And so it was, for Lann later gave birth to a son in Dublin, who they called Eysteinn. He succeeded Olafr as king of Dublin.

Auisle, who had come along with other Jarls, pushed himself into the presence of Aed, Olafr and his bride, and crudely commented, "If you are to wrestle with her every night, you won't be much good in the fight, but then you have already practised in the Hebrides". Olafr was deeply offended that he should have made such a remark in the presence of his new wife and her father.

It was not long after the wedding that news came of Malachy's move into Aed's territory. The Norse and Danish forces had arrived in time, and the combined forces were quickly assembled to meet the challenge. They met in open ground, and Aed sent word that he wished to talk to Malachy who then invited him into his camp.

Malachy spoke directly, "You know why I have come into the field – to receive your submission to me as High King or to destroy you in battle."

Aed responded, "Our forces look very well matched and that may not be as easy as you imagine".

Malachy became angry, "You dare to start by defying me, allied as you are with the Heathen."

At this the Abbott joined in, threatening Aed with excommunication and damnation for his association with the Norse and Danes. Matters became very heated and Aed began to think he would not get out of the camp alive and that it had been a mistake to think he could negotiate with Malachy. Under such pressure, Aed agreed to swear allegiance to Malachy on holy relics in the presence of the Abbott of Armagh. Aed then returned to his forces that were camped alongside those of Malachy for the night.

Aed told Flann, Ivarr and Olafr what had occurred and how he had been forced into submission.

Olafr responded, "You have your forces intact and your opponents sleep soundly in a sense of security. Let us attack them whilst they are disadvantaged".

Aed knew if he was to become the High King, he had to take the initiative whilst the chance was there, and he had the Viking forces with him. His swearing allegiance on the holy relics did not prove to be any deterrence to his agreement.

Aed and his allies prepared their forces to attack Malachy's camp once the talk had died down and the fires had turned to embers. Most of Malachy's camp was asleep in their tents. The night was dark and

Ivarr was concerned as to how he would be able to control his men and react to situations as they developed. It would not be possible to fight using shield walls or use the arrowhead formation against standing forces, nor could they use their bowmen. It would be a general free for all in the dark. The only suggestion he could offer was that the camp should be surrounded before the attack and all would move in against the tents nearest to them. This was agreed, and on the blow of the horn, the attack began. The element of surprise saw an initial success as Malachy's men struggled to get out of their tents and were easily attacked, but a resolute resistance developed in the darkness and Aed's men were scattered about and unable to build a shield wall in the confusion that followed. Eventually Aed's forces broke in disarray and returned to their own camp. They were not pursued. The next day, Malachy remained well established in Aed's territory but showed no inclination to follow up with an attack. Eventually he returned home and his health began to deteriorate.

During the fight with Malachy's men, in the dark and confusion, Finn and Gunnr found themselves in a very dangerous situation with friend and foe both before and behind them. It was difficult to distinguish between them, and their skills in battle could not be fully utilised in the dark. The fight came down to one of luck not skill, and Gunnr became a victim as he was stabbed in the back and fell to the ground. Finn saw him fall but all he could do at the time was to protect himself from the assaults of the enemy. As the battle moved to and fro, Finn was able to pull Gunnr clear of the field and tie up his wound to slow the bleeding. He then helped him back to the camp, as the rest of their forces retreated under the orders of Ivarr. Gunnr was weak from loss of blood, and later developed an infection causing a high fever. Finn obtained salt to try to clean the wound, but Gunnr looked near to death as he was taken back to Dublin. There he was delivered into the hands of the women. Finn was instructed by his Jarl to join him in the raids that followed and he left with a heavy heart fearing the death of his friend.

Aed, Olafr and Ivarr then raided deep into Malachy's territory. They were unopposed. The following year they were joined by Flann and again were unopposed. Malachy died in that year of 862, on November 29th, a wet and miserable day. Malachy had spent his life trying to unite and hold together the Christian kings of Erin but it was in his death that unity came. On the stone seat at Tullahoge in County Tyrone, Aed was crowned High King before all the kings of Erin who submitted to him.

Aed's elevation to High King cut off the Norse and Danish access to plunder, which could not be gained without breaking their alliance. Ivarr and Olafr were concerned as to how they could retain the loyalty of their followers without rewards and discussed their options at length.

"We cannot afford to unite the whole of the Irish against us," said Ivarr. "Our options are becoming more limited every day as monks build their defensive round towers some over ninety feet high."

These towers were built of stone with a door twelve feet above the ground and only one narrow window on each floor, each window looking in different directions. A single moveable ladder provided access between each floor. The towers had originally been built as belfries and were then adapted to be a very effective defensive structure.

Olafr suggested they look at the Boyne burial mounds, where he thought treasure must have been buried with the entombed kings. However they were sited in Flann's territory, in the vicinity of Knowth, the main fortress in northern Brega. Ivarr was hesitant to undertake the raid, but agreed when he learnt that Lorcan, the King of Mide, had originated the plan and wanted to take part.

The tombs were believed by the Irish to be the home of Oengus, the god of the underworld, and where the fairy mistress of the kings of Tara lived. Despite the sacred nature of the tombs, Flann did nothing to oppose the invasion of his territory. All the tombs were dug up and searched, including one stone passage ninety feet long leading to its inner chamber. The caves of Knowth, Newgrange, and Boadan's Grave over Dowth were desecrated, along with the cave of the Smith's wife. The work involved had been lengthy and laborious but yielded nothing. They were unaware of the prehistoric age of the burials. A disappointed army of men wearily returned to Dublin to reappraise their future.

Word came back of the hostility held by Aed because of the destruction of the Boyne tombs and he showed it by invading the territory of King Lorcan of Mide, whom he captured and blinded. The Viking leaders immediately held a council to decide how to react.

Ivarr was the first to speak saying, "I no longer see profit for our armies in Ireland and do not want a prolonged war with the united Irish kings, which would deplete our resources to little gain. From our Dublin base, we can make better use of our armies in the rich kingdoms in England those of Strathclyde and Pictland. I have good knowledge from my sources of the state of the kingdom of North Humberland, which is in civil war, with King Osbert being driven out by a usurper called Aelle. I have thrown the runes and found it propitious for us to invade".

Olafr was still fascinated by the stories of Aussle, and the chance to ally with the Scots against the Picts, being influenced by the knowledge that his son Thorsteinn was active in Sutherland, Argyll and Caithness in the north, carving out a kingdom in Pictish territory.

Olafr responded, "Let us divide our forces. I will go with Aussle and make an alliance with the Scots in the west, before going into Pictland. You go into North Humberland from the east and we can then combine our forces to take the British kingdom of Strathclyde. If we attack their fortress at Dumbarton on the River Clyde, we can thus secure access from the River Forth on the east coast by hauling our ships across land to the River Clyde, then connecting the east to our base in Dublin and avoid the perilous voyage north about".

Ivarr thought long and deeply about how to achieve his aims and the resources he would require. Knowing he would need horses and to ensure surprise of attack in North Humberland, he planned to start his campaign to the south in East Anglia, a low lying land full of inland fens and waterways easily penetrated by his long ships. He had learnt much about the kingdom of East Anglia during his stay on the island of Sheppey in the Thames estuary. He knew of the rich farmlands and the availability of livestock for provisions and access to horses for which they were famous, and which he planned to take as danegeld. He decided he would split his forces by sea and by land in his assault on Northumbria. And so the conquest of England and the creation of Scotland began.

Finn, on returning to Dublin, had found his friend Gunnr in a desperate condition, with his eyes sunken into their sockets, and lying pale and lifeless. He washed his wound and encouraged him to eat, for which he had no taste. He then went to see a seeress called Thorbjorg, who was skilled in magic rites and in foreseeing the future. Finn paid for her services to weave her magic on Gunnr, who was placed on a raised platform with Thorbjorg. Around the platform the ward enticers formed a ring. These were women who sang the ward songs to bring the spirits into the circle. Thorbjorg closed her eyes and went into a semi trance, chanting the magic words and lapsing into silence. It was a long time before she opened her eyes and spoke, "Gunnr will recover and will fight many battles. He will become a leader and will gain wealth."

Finn was encouraged by this and stayed with Gunnr to aid his recovery. He paid for herbs and medicines to be applied by the ward enticers. And so it happened, slowly over time his suppurating wound dried up and the skin healed. However it was many months before he regained his weight and strength. By the time Ivarr was ready to sail to East Anglia, Gunnr was fully recovered and ready to fight.

Chapter 6

BJORN IRONSIDE IN FRANCE

In the year 854AD, on leaving his brother Ivarr on the Isle of Thanet, Bjorn sailed back to France with the ships under his command, accompanied by Hastein and his fleet. They joined the Vikings on the River Seine and were in turn joined by the leader Sidroc who had been campaigning on the River Loire. They were successful in ravaging the surrounding areas of the river as far upstream as Pitres but Charles the Bald managed to check them at La Perche. Bjorn and Hastein went back down the river and refortified the island of Oissel near the mouth of the river whilst Sidroc decided to go back to the River Loire. The next year Bjorn and Hastein left their ships behind and went up the banks of the river by horse, meeting no opposition. They made a winter raid on Paris, and were paid a heavy ransom after burning down the churches of St. Peter and St. Paul.

Lothair II, the great grandson of Charles the Great, had by now abandoned Frisia to the Vikings from where they would launch their raids. Nevertheless he approached Charles the Bald to enter into a joint defence pact. Charles was wily and insisted that the first attack should be in his territory against the Seine Vikings on the island of Oissel. In July he raised not only a large army but a fleet of ships as well. He was also joined by the king of Aquitaine, a younger king also called Charles, along with the army of Lothair II.

Despite their overwhelming strength and a fleet to carry them on to the island, their courage did not match their advantage. They decided not to attack the strong fortifications fearing heavy losses but, instead, began a blockade from which the Vikings could not break out. The Viking long ships had been brought inside the fortification, to avoid their seizure and could not be easily launched without being attacked. The river itself had been blockaded to prevent escape to sea. After a three-month blockade, with provisions running out, Bjorn and Hastein were becoming increasingly desperate with few options open to them. They daily discussed what to do.

Bjorn asked, "Here we sit in our prison looking out to the freedom of the seas. Are we to die of starvation here, or should we die like men in battle?"

Hastein responded, "We would indeed die in battle with such strong forces barricaded on land and the sea blockade taking away any advantage of our fleet. We could negotiate unfavourable terms if Charles was prepared to negotiate but I fear it would signal our weakness and encourage the blockade. We must hold our nerve and await our fate." And so they agreed.

Unknown to them however, the disunity and fragmentation of the dynasty following Charles the Great's death continued to cause the slow decline of the empire. Lewis, the German, had raised an army to check the Slavs and Abodriti. At this point in time disaffected Frankish nobles had approached Lewis to complain bitterly about the tyranny of Charles the Bald. Lewis, believing he had sufficient support, was persuaded to intervene against his half brother and overthrow him, causing Charles to rapidly withdraw to meet the threat. Bjorn and Hastein watched in disbelief as the large army decamped and the ships departed, a lifeline they did not expect to happen.

"This is one hap that no one could have foreseen," said Bjorn, "we are fortunate to have survived."

Hastein was more circumspect, "Did I not say we should hold our nerve, it always comes down to a question of who has the strongest will."

The armies of Charles and Lewis met at Brienne, but Charles suspected the loyalty of his generals and decided to negotiate rather than attack. After three days of negotiations, Charles left his army in place but retreated to Burgundy where he raised a further army. Faced with fresh forces, and with the Bishops now declaring their support for Charles, Lewis was obliged to retreat and deal with the Slavs.

Bjorn was unsettled by the way things were going and the narrow escape they had been granted by fate. He was aware of Charles' machinations with other Vikings and his willingness to play one band off against the other with bribes. Bjorn was also acutely aware of Charles' blockade of the rivers and the fortifying of the banks, particularly at Pitres just above the island of Oissel and below the confluence of the Rivers Eure and Andelle, which cut off these waterways to their ships. He concluded that the runes did not augur well for the Seine Viking's future prospects.

Bjorn decided he would try to do a deal with Charles whilst his fleet and plunder was still intact. Charles was similarly unsettled by his failure to dislodge the Vikings at the island of Oissel and the threat to his flank from his own relations. Bjorn met Charles at Verberie and began discussions that quickly bore fruit. He was granted tracts of land for himself and his men near the coast, conditional upon their defence of the surrounding regions from other Vikings and his abandonment of the island of Oissel.

Bjorn's instincts to negotiate with Charles had been right. The Seine Vikings continued to attack Paris, so in 860AD Charles approached the Vikings on the Somme led by Weland, asking them to dislodge the Seine Vikings. He offered hostages and a payment of 3,000 pounds of silver. Part of the silver was slow to arrive so Weland left with his hostages to fight in England where he attacked Winchester. However he was defeated by the men of Wessex and returned to France to renegotiate his deal with Charles. This time he was given

5,000 pounds of silver plus cattle and corn and honoured his deal by blockading the Seine Vikings in their island prison. Being on the point of starvation, and knowing that Weland was made of stronger metal whose determination would not waver, they gave up 6,000 pounds of gold and silver to be allowed to have the freedom of the sea, a large part of the plunder they had gathered over the years.

Whilst at court, Bjorn became aware of the divisions in the family and the rebellious nature of his sons. The eldest son was Lewis the Stammerer, the dissolution of whose marriage to Ansgard was caused by the interference of his father who wanted him to marry the daughter of the king of the Bretons. This caused Lewis great resentment against his father. The Bretons had been a problem to Charles until Salomon became king who had agreed to pay tribute to Charles in 857AD. Lewis the Stammerer led a force of Bretons in 862AD to attack Robert the Strong's territory of Anjou but Robert supported Charles the Bald and defeated Lewis, forcing his submission.

The second son was Charles king of Acquitaine. He also married against his father's wishes when fifteen years old. However he was killed in 866AD when on a hunting expedition. He decided to play a joke on a companion who had strayed away from the hunting party. He pretended to attack him but the companion did not recognise him in the dusk and killed him.

The third son was Lothair who was put into a religious order as was the fourth son Carloman who rebelled against the order. For his trouble Carloman was arrested, tried and blinded but managed to escape to his uncle Lewis the German. Charles' daughter Judith was at this time married to King Aethelbald of Wessex.

Judith had been the child bride of King Aethelwulf of Wessex. On Aethelwulf's death and despite his antipathy towards the marriage of his father, the succeeding King Aethelbald also married Judith, creating a scandal among the West Saxons. When Aethelbald died after four years, Judith returned to her father's court in 863AD, a wilful and striking woman who had entered into a relationship with one of Charles' soldiers, a man distinguished by his actions in his army. He was called Baldwin the Forrester. Judith had given every encouragement to Baldwin and when, supposedly carried off by force, she was only too eager to become his wife. Charles forbade the marriage. But, on threats by Baldwin to go over to the Vikings who had the support of Charles' son Lewis the Stammerer and mindful of his own experience and the support of the Pope, Charles gave his permission to the marriage though he didn't attend it.

Bjorn settled down on his new lands and started a family but, like his brothers, he was ever restless for action and became bored. He brooded on the voyage he had taken with his brothers Ivarr, Halfdan and Ubbe sailing around Spain as far as the Pillars of Hercules and attacking Lisbon and Seville. He had heard about the southern part of the Frankish empire dipping into the Mediterranean Sea and the treasures of Italy and his imagination was fired by what opportunities for profit might lay in the Mediterranean Sea beyond the Pillars of Hercules. His plans to make such an adventurous voyage matured over time until he decided to discuss his ambitions with Hastein. Once together, their enthusiasm for the venture grew apace and they decided to increase their fleets by building new ships to bring the fleet up to seventy ships. This was accomplished in very quick time.

Setting out from the River Loire, they sailed past the Viking's base on the island of Noirmoutier to cross the Bay of Biscay. Heavy seas were rolling in from the Atlantic, making life on board very uncomfortable until they reached the deeper waters to the north of Spain off Asturias, which they unwisely decided to attack. King Ordono was busy with the constant need to fight the Arabs encroaching north. However the mountainous people of Asturia were hardy men and Count Don Pedro raised enough men to attack and defeat the Viking raiders. In the frenzied activity of defence and trying to get back on to the ships, Don Pedro's men managed to capture and disable several ships. This was not a good start to the venture but, undeterred, the fleet sailed around northwest Spain and south towards the lands held by the Arabs where they encountered the Arab ships guarding the coasts. The Viking attack on the Arab ships, which were thwarting their attempts to land, again proved no easy task and two further ships were lost in the process. Abandoning further attempts to land they continued on to Southern Spain and entered the River Guadalquivir bound by the orange groves until they were able to see the minarets of Seville that they intended to attack. However an army led by Hajib Isa-ibn-Hassan halted their progress. Bjorn and Hastein wisely retreated to the sea.

Having been repulsed three times, they decided to go through the Pillars of Hercules into the Mediterranean Sea, something no other Viking had attempted. As they approached the straits, a heat haze obscured their visibility. They kept close to the Spanish shore in sight of the white chalk cliffs, thus making a safe passage through the straits. The wind and tide flowing in from the Atlantic Ocean made for rapid progress into the Mediterranean, propelling them into the unknown with unseemly haste. The Vikings were not intimidated, emerging into this vast unknown sea and facing the peoples and circumstances they might find. With the confidence and assurance of their race, they made surprise attacks on all the coastal settlements in the province of Malaga that they came across, moving forward like the wind from one attack to another, burning mosques and taking plunder. They were met by Arab troops but managed to gain a victory over them until the Emir himself raised so large an army that the Vikings were forced to leave the Spanish coast and sail south to Africa. The Arabs had been successful in driving the Visigoths out of Spain and they had then settled the lands conquered before going on to threaten Francia itself. The Viking threat from a northern race, mobile and equally skilled in seamanship, was a rude awakening to them.

Bjorn and Hastein arrived at Nekor in Morocco, which they attacked. The king of the Moors raised an army to check the Vikings and marched to encounter them, camping for the night before an attack. However the king, having seen these strange tall confident men in their armour ruthlessly sacking the town and, undeterred by his army's presence, became full of doubt and he fled in the night. His army finding itself leaderless in the cold light of the morning panicked and also fled, leaving the Vikings to their task and their citizens at their mercy.

Bjorn and Hastein were now buoyed up by their success, and decided again to attack the province of Malaga. They were successful in defeating the local coastal defenders, and then sailed northeast passed Alicante but the Arab fleet intercepted them and they lost two more ships. Continuing on they saw the Balearic Islands and harried widely in the islands of Ibiza, Mallorca and Menorca, before sailing north to reach the northeast coast of Spain, areas never before exposed to such ravages. They captured King Garcia of Navarre and received a large ransom before sailing on to take Narbonne in Francia. They reached the delta of the River Rhone and the marshy Camargue, a natural place to shelter and replenish their supplies and provisions and to repair their ships, making sure they were well fortified whilst about their work. Before moving on, they sailed up the river Rhone deep into Francia to take Valence, in the territory of Charles the King of Provence, and third son of the King of Lotheringia, Lothair II. Ever an opportunist and always prepared to gain territory at the expense of the empire's unity, Charles the Bald seized the chance to invade Provence whilst they were under threat from the Vikings.

Bjorn and Hastein then set their eye on reaching Italy and taking Rome, the city they had heard so much about. The scale of their ambitions grew from the confidence they had in their own abilities, despite the fact they had no pilots or knowledge of Italy nor knew the location of Rome. As they turned south down the western side of Italy, they saw a city with gleaming white walls, which they assumed must be Rome. In fact it was the city of La Luna.

As the ships drifted, Bjorn and Hastein discussed how best to attack such a well-fortified city without sacrificing many lives. It was Hastein, ever the most devious and cunning of the leaders, who put forward a strategy.

"These people are Christians, who will know little about us or our beliefs, let us be canny and by guile we can trick them," said Hastein. "Let us pretend we are Christians driven away by our fellow Christians in Francia and that I am dying and in need of spiritual help and blessing. Then let me die and for you to seek my burial inside the city in Christian ground"

Bjorn replied laughingly, "This might well work but the planning will need to be very exact to avoid you being buried alive."

Hastein was laid on a stretcher and his face and hands were lightly coloured by a mixture of chalk, ashes and carbon, to give him the grey appearance of the dying, but well wrapped to avoid close inspection. Bjorn and a few Vikings approached the city gates carrying Hastein, and speaking in French, he related the agreed story line. The Bishop of La Luna was called and with his priests, blessed Hastein and sprinkled holy water upon him, with Bjorn concerned that the water would fall on Hastein's face and wash off the ash. Hastein was returned to the ship, and the next day in late afternoon, he was enclosed in white cloths and again taken to the gates. Bjorn advised them of the death of their king and his wish to be buried in Christian ground. The Governor and the Bishop agreed to allow in the dead king, with his mourners, who were then led in solemn procession towards the monastery. The priests sang the mass for the dead but, before they could bury him, the Vikings called out that he must be burned and, at this signal, Hastein leaped up, with all drawing their swords and cutting down any man who stood in their way in the rush to hold the gates. The Vikings outside the wall had cleverly concealed themselves and had just enough time to gain the gates before any reinforcements arrived to prevent them entering the town. The town was quickly overcome and sacked and provided a great deal of treasure.

The fleet, now fully laden with all manner of treasure, began the long journey home, arriving back in the year 866AD. Bjorn returned to his lands, his thirst for adventure now sated, but Hastein was again soon in his old haunts. In the autumn of that year, he assembled a troop of some 400 Danes and some Bretons to attack Le Mans on the River Sarthe, a tributary of the River Loire. They had galloped across country to effect surprise but, on their return, Count Robert the Strong and Count Ramnulf had raised a large army of Frankish warriors far outnumbering Hastein's band who were intercepted at Brisarthe. Ever quick thinking, Hastein led his men into a stone church, with those who did not make it being cut down by the Franks. The Franks made many fruitless attempts to dislodge them but, in the end, decided to camp outside. The Franks relaxed their guard, and Count Robert took off his helmet. Hastein, ever the man to seize the initiative, led a mock charge against the Franks, whose superior numbers slowly drove them back to the church door where they again made a stand and where Count Robert without his helmet was killed. Count Ramnulf was also hit with an arrow fired from the church window, causing him to die two days later. With Count Robert dead and Count Ramnulf dying, the Franks lost all heart and allowed the Vikings to slip away.

With yet another close encounter with death, Hastein began to come round to the view that it was time he too should be bought off. He was given land at Chartres to protect the frontier from other Vikings and became a trusted Councillor to the king of Francia.

In 880AD Rolf the Ganger with his fleet had invaded France, proving a particular problem to the king of Francia. Hastein was eventually sent to negotiate with Rolf on behalf of the king, and on their meeting Rolf had challenged him as to who he was.

Hastein replied, "Heard ye never of Hastein?"

Rolf replied, "Yea, we have heard of him as the man who began well and ended ill."

Rolf was a Norseman from the Orkney Isles who was so tall his feet were near the ground when he rode a horse, and so he was named Rolf the Ganger. He was eventually given Normandy on condition that he prevented other Vikings sailing into the king of France's territory. It was Rolf's descendants in Normandy led by William the Conqueror, Duke of Normandy, who in 1066AD defeated the English King Harold at the battle of Hastings which changed forever the history of England.

Chapter 7

THE CONQUEST OF

NORTHUMBRIA AND EAST ANGLIA

Planning his conquest of Northumbria, Ivarr sent word of his intentions to mount a major campaign in England to the Vikings at Noirmoutier, the island base at the mouth of the River Loire in France and requested support from their fleets. Word came back from Sidroc that he would support the campaign, and Ivarr arranged for the combined fleets to join up off East Anglia to finalize details of the campaign in 865AD. Ivarr had chosen East Anglia for his winter quarters, where he would prepare and provision his forces, far enough away from Northumbria to ensure complete surprise. He intended his campaign to be swift and effective. The need for horses was an essential requirement for this.

King Edmund of East Anglia was advised of the Danish fleet lying off the coast at the mouth of the river Stour. A force was sent to ascertain their strength and intent.

Ivarr sent a herald to speak to them, saying, "My venerable Lord Ivarr, the unconquerable king and terror by land and sea who has by force of arms subjected countries to his rule, has landed on your desirable shores with a great fleet, intent on establishing his winter quarters here."

King Edmund's representative, Eadric replied, "What is your reason for wintering on our shores. Have you come in peace and when do you intend to leave?"

The herald responded, "We seek provisions for the winter and have no warlike intent on your kingdom. We will go north into Mercia in the summer and we will need horses for our transport." Eadric said that he would return with an answer to their request.

Eadric reported to the king and his councillors.

"My Lord they have a mighty fleet, fully manned with armed warriors, well equipped and capable and led by Ivarr the King of Dublin, who we know in years past has caused great suffering from his island base of Sheppey in the River Thames. I fear they could do great damage to your kingdom and could conquer our lands with such a mighty force."

King Edmund was a devout Christian and not hasty for war, preferring compromise, and so he addressed his councillors.

"As a Christian, I will not submit to a Pagan king but, as other English kings have found, it is more expedient to pay danegeld, than to sacrifice life in an uncertain outcome. The provision of food and horses is a small price to pay for their departure from our shores, though I fear for those at their destination."

The Danish fleet moved into the River Stour, anchoring and beaching their ships, before setting up a defensive camp. Ivarr, with his brothers Halfdan and Ubbe, and with the other Viking leaders, Sidroc and later joined by Osketil, Baegseg and Guthorm from the Rivers Seine and the Rhine, planned their strategy over the winter. Ivarr, always a leader to plan carefully and thoroughly but who, when he was satisfied as to the outcome, would move at lightning speed. He felt he needed more information about the civil war taking place in Nothumbria, between King Osberht and the usurper Aelle. It had raged for three years and weakened the kingdom. He not only sent his spies into Northumbria, mixing with the Danish traders in York, but he himself travelled into the kingdom to assess the defences, the logistical problems of the route and the need to maintain surprise. It was not until the following autumn that Ivarr felt the time was ready to move. He sent his fleet north to the mouth of the River Humber, whilst the army with the horses provided by King Edmund rode north along the old Roman roads, through Lincoln and on to a meeting point on the south bank of the River Humber, where Grimsby was to be built by the Danes in later times. The army arrived ahead of the fleet and kept a low profile until the ships arrived. The ships then ferried the men and horses across to the northern bank of the River Humber, just west of the spur of land they named Holderness. Thus the marshy areas to the west of the wide Humber estuary were avoided, for though nearer to York, the loss of time and possible surprise was too great a risk. Some ships were left at anchor in the protection of the spur of land and out of harm's way from any counter attack. Ivarr left enough men to move the ships should the need arise. The rest of the fleet moved up the River Humber, turning north into the tributary of the River Ouse until they reached York carrying those fighting men who did not have horses.

Gunnr and Finn had not ridden horses before. The journey north had not been a comfortable one as they became sore and stiff from riding without stirrups. Eventually they learnt to grip the horses' belly and lift themselves up to the rhythm of the horses' movements. It had been necessary to stop at places to water and graze the horses regularly and they had been glad of the respite. As their muscles adjusted to their new exercise, they became adept riders by the time they reached the mouth of the River Humber. The chestnut coloured horses were stocky and not much bigger than ponies. Loading the horses on to the ships had been a difficult task. They had a limited number of Knorr ships designed to carry livestock and cargo. Gunnr's horse began to panic and lash out as he tried to load him.

"Yours is a very skittish hoss," laughed Finn, "I hope you haven't told him about our shipwreck," as Gunnr struggled to calm him down before he damaged himself or the ship.

The skill of loading was in the mastery of the horse and driving it forward up the gangway at speed. The river with its wide estuary was the largest they had ever seen. They had blindfolded the horses to keep them quiet on crossing.

From the north bank the mounted army rode at all speed to York, taking it completely by surprise and meeting little resistance, capturing it on November 1st 866AD, during the feast of All Saints when the city's guard was at its lowest. Ivarr, who knew that King Osberht and Aelle were both still in the field, prepared for a counter attack. The Roman walls, though strong, were crumbling and could be breached by a determined force, since they were very long and would be difficult to man fully. He set about building inner defences and killing zones within the walls, and sent out men to watch the approaches and forewarn of any advance by the Northumbrians. Ivarr set out to play down the size of his force and planned to lure the Northumbrians inside the walls where his hidden forces would attack without mercy. Gunnr and Finn worked hard on the defences, which had time to be thoroughly built as the Northumbrians were slow to react. They lived well on the roasted cattle and sheep taken from the surrounding countryside. Gunnr, in exploring the city, found a hoard of silver coins loosely hidden. Both he and Finn had begun to amass wealth from their military exploits and hoped to purchase a ship one day. Finn retrieved an axe decoratively designed with a silver inlay. During this period they could relax, safe in comfortable surroundings and they came to know the Northumbrians who were similar to the Danish Vikings, being descended mainly from Angles and Jutes originating in Denmark.

It was not until the following spring that King Osberht and Aelle had settled their differences to the point where they could work together against the Danes, a period of time allowing Ivarr to be fully prepared. On March 21st 867AD, their combined forces marched on York. Ivarr, being forewarned, sent a small force out of the gates to meet them as they approached. The force made a feint attack before retreating back through the gates and the Northumbrians emboldened rushed through the gates behind them. Once inside, the gates were shut and Ivarr's full force was brought to bear, killing all inside. Both King Osberht and Aelle were among those killed.

With the Northumbrian army defeated, the Danes plundered widely, moving north to the River Tyne and the northern part of the kingdom called Bernicia, which submitted without a fight. Ivarr appointed a Saxon called Egberht as a vassal king to look after his interests in Bernicia. Archbishop Wulfhere also collaborated with the Danes and supported the vassal king. Ubbe was left in Northumbria to consolidate their hold on the kingdom they had won whilst Ivarr, with Halfdan, led his forces south into Mercia in the winter of 868AD. Here they took advantage of the wide deep River Trent flowing north into the River Humber and, rowing upstream to the south between the low lying banks bordered by flat meadows and lined by willows, they arrived at Nottingham. This was taken with little resistance for use as their winter quarters and they fortified it.

King Burgred of Mercia, married to Aethelswyth a West Saxon princess, called on the help of the West Saxon King Aethelred and his twenty-year old younger brother, Alfred, who was married to the daughter of the Mercian Ealdorman, Aethelred. They also sent a messenger to King Edmund of East Anglia requesting his support. King Edmund consulted his councillors and bishops and, after considering their views, he made his decision.

"My Christian conscience will not allow me to break the terms of my peace agreed with the Danes who, like us, are Angles and I cannot therefore send support to King Burgred."

The messenger returned to relay a decision that boded ill for the Angles in West Mercia and indeed those of East Anglia. However, the combined armies of Wessex and Mercia marched to Nottingham but, conscious of the fate of the Northumbrians and without the experience of using siege engines against impregnable walls, they decided to blockade the city. Ivarr, seeing that he was heavily outnumbered, decided not to offer battle but sat within the city's walls to wait events. Using his cunning, he knew that the Saxons had no standing army and they would want to tend their fields in the spring and he also knew that such a large army camped outside would draw heavily on provisions and supplies. He started by trying to negotiate terms that indicated he was prepared to leave Nottingham in the summer when he had plans in the north and that he wanted to remain where he was for his winter quarters. Before the effects of starvation could bring about submission, the Saxons offered terms to allow the Danes to leave in peace that included a financial payment to the Danes. Ivarr was pleased to accept terms given in his favour despite being surrounded by a large and superior army and so returned to York without harm. From this time on, the Mercian King Burgred lost the initiative and was soon under the domination of the Danes. He was later forced to flee to Rome with his wife (Alfred's sister Aethelswith) and he died soon after.

Ivarr, with the army of Wessex returning back over the River Thames, decided to winter his troops again in East Anglia and sent his fleet south. The fleet disembarked part of the army on the coast north of Great Yarmouth for them to march to Thetford. This was the capital of East Anglia and surrounded by rich farmland known as the Brecklands. The city contained palaces and religious houses, situated on the Little Ouse, a navigable tributary of the River Ouse flowing through the low lying marshy land into the Wash. They then sailed on to a safe anchorage at the mouth of the River Stour when the remaining army on board disembarked, to make their way to Thetford. Meanwhile Halfdan had stayed behind with a smaller part of the army when the fleet departed with the intent of invading East Mercia. No longer fearing King Burgred's smaller forces which, in

the event, did not offer battle, the plan was to plunder
the way to East Anglia and Thetford. Having crosse
bank of the River Humber on his ships, he marched
Lincoln, diverting to sack the monastery at Bardeney.
south down the old Roman road until they camped at
called Launden south of Sleaford, which was later known as
Threekingham. Here they threw up earth mounds and wooden
defences and began plundering the surrounding areas. Abandoned by
King Burgred, the local Ealdormen raised what forces they could.
Ealdorman Morcar of Bourne, and Ealdormen Algar of Holland who
had distinguished himself in the eyes of the king in the siege of
Nottingham along with Osgod the Shire Reeve of Lincoln, came
together with forces raised by a monk called Toli from Crowland
Abbey plus men from Deeping and Baston. Toli had been a warrior
in the past, achieving distinction. Harding of Ryhall also came with a
band of fighting men from Stamford. Marching on the Dane's camp
they not only surprised them but also considerably outnumbered
them. The Danes were thrown back into a defensive position inside
their camp and three of the Jarls were killed. Try as they might, they
could not dislodge the Danes and, as night fell, they camped outside.
In the night, the larger part of Halfdan's forces returned to the camp
with, Baegseg and Osketil. Many Mercians slipped away in fear in
the night. The next day the Danes came out to fight and the Mercians
formed a tight wedge shaped shield wall to withstand the attacks
from arrows, spears and horse charges. They stood firm, even with
the Berserkers cursing and ranting until rage overcame them, when
they would drive themselves into the shield wall to try to break
through. As the day wore on with little headway being made by the
Danes, they began to withdraw and the Mercians broke ranks only to
find the Danes turn around and attack with their full force. The shield
wall fragmented and individual bands of men were set upon and
killed. Toli reformed his men and stood firm on some higher ground
at Stow Green which was difficult to find in such a flat landscape
but, he too was worn down and his men slain. Those who could

did so fleeing towards Morkery wood and three men from
ton and Gedney took the news back to Crowland Abbey.

Crowland Abbey had been sited on an island on which the hermit
Saint Guthlac had lived. He was a member of the royal family of
Mercia. He had become a recluse at the age of twenty-six in 699AD
and died there fifteen years later. He was a visionary and Aethelbald
the Great, Nephew of King Penda, had come to him as a fugitive
from Celred to seek his advice. On Saint Guthlac's death he appeared
to Aethelbald in a vision and told him he would be king of Mercia
within a year by divine providence. When Aethelbald became king he
built the Abbey on the island of Crowland after Saint Guthlac's
death. The land, accessed by a bridge, was surrounded by four rivers
and could not bear the weight of stone so they had to pile the ground
with beech and oak and bring in earth by boat.

On hearing the ill news, the Abbot Theodore of Crowland Abbey
celebrated Matins and then dismissed all thirty able-bodied monks to
safe keeping in the fens. They went by boat to the wood of Ancarig
staying there for four days. They took with them their relics, charters
and precious effects, along with the body of Saint Guthlac with his
Psalter and scourge. Some of the older monks decided to stay with
the young boy novices in the face of the encroaching smoke from
fires moving towards them. The Danes were advancing south, after
they had raised three mounds to bury the dead Jarls at Threekingham.
Other articles of value such as cups and vessels were thrown down
the cloister well but the altar, containing the gold plate presented by
King Whitlaf, was visible above the water. Theodore and two elderly
monks pulled it up and hid it elsewhere in the woods but it has never
been found. The Abbot was conducting mass assisted by Elfgy his
Deacon and the candle bearers as the Danes burst in. Osketil rushed
forward and killed Abbot Theodore. The other monks were killed
without mercy after being tortured to reveal where the treasure lay. A
boy aged ten years called Thurgar followed the prior Lethwyn into

the refectory. When he saw the prior killed, he pleaded to be killed alongside him. Sidroc was moved to spare him, putting his cloak over the boy as a sign of his protection. He was thus saved, though taken as a slave. The marble tombs were broken open with ploughshares in a search for treasure, including that of Saint Guthlac but they found nothing. After three days the Abbey was burnt down and continued to burn for fourteen days.

The Danes moved on with a large herd of cattle to Medeshampstead. In 655AD Peada, son of the Mercian King Penda, had founded a monastery there. At its later rebuilding by Ethelwold, Bishop of Winchester, it was called Peterborough after the Cathedral of Saint Peter. Here the Abbey walls were well built and the gates shut. It required siege equipment by the Danes to scale them. A monk dropped a large stone on the head of a Jarl in the process of gaining entry to the Abbey. Inevitably the Abbey was taken and burnt for fifteen days and every monk was slain. On moving south towards the Abbey at Huntingdon, circumventing the vast Fenlands stretching to the east, two of the wagons containing treasure slipped off a stone bridge when crossing over the River Nene. In the confusion, the young boy, Thurgar saved by Sidroc, was able to escape into a wood and walked through the night back to Crowland Abbey. The young monks had returned and were putting out the flames. They were overcome with tears on discovering the deaths of their companions. On lifting the roof timbers off the altar they discovered the body of the Abbot with his head chopped off and partially burnt. Two of the elderly monks had had their hands cut off in the chapter house. After the monastery had been cleared of debris they elected Godric as the new Abbott. They then went to Medeshampstead to give a Christian burial to the monks there. Eighty-four monks were buried in a common grave upon the feast of Saint Cecilia, covered by a pyramid of stones, on which a stone carving depicted the Abbot and his monks. Each year thereafter they would go to the site to say mass and pray for the souls interred therein.

Huntingdon Abbey was next, followed by the Bishop's Palace at Cambridge, both suffering the same fate as Medehampstead Abbey. From Cambridge, they crossed the River Cam into East Anglia and reached the southern part of the fens before continuing northeast on the way to Thetford. On seeing the majestic walls of the monastery on the Isle of Ely, a vast island surrounded by water and elevated above the flat reed beds trembling in the wind, they followed a causeway over the shallow water and crossed the River Ouse on to the island. This monastery too was plundered and burnt.

On meeting up with their fellow Danes at Thetford, Ivarr learnt that the East Anglians had attacked them but they had driven them off and killed their leader, Ealdorman Ulfcetil. Ivarr then sent word to King Edmund that he should submit to him and pay tribute of half the king's treasures or face the conquest of his kingdom. King Edmund, knowing his position was weak against such a strong army camped in his territory was prepared to submit to Ivarr but, in conscience, could not do so to a Pagan king. He sent word back to Ivarr with his messenger.

"Know therefore, that for the love of this earthly life, Edmund the Christian king will not submit to a heathen Chief unless he renounces his gods and is baptised as a Christian."

Ivarr, steeped in the traditions and practice of his Pagan Gods, was angered by the suggestion and he took his army east from Thetford to plunder East Anglia. King Edmund led his men into the field and the armies met at Hoxne. The East Anglians were quickly routed and King Edmund was taken captive. The Danes stripped him naked, and then tied him to a tree. His sacrifice to Odin began with an arrow shot into his leg. King Edmund cried out to Christ in his agony and so he was mocked with the Danes asking where was his Christ coming to save him. Other arrows were then shot at him aimed at his extremities and as he writhed in agony he called upon his God. Ivarr then instructed him to be cut down and whilst still alive the ceremony of the blood eagle was carried out with his ribs being cut from his spine and his lungs pulled out. His head was then cut off with an axe and later cast into the bushes at Hellesdon wood and he became a martyr on November 20th in the year 869AD. The Bishops later built two chapels, one where King Edmund was martyred and called Hoxne Priory and the other was built a mile from Hoxne where King Edmund's head was cast into the bushes in the wood. When it was found, the East Anglians claimed that a wolf had stood guard over the head.

The East Anglians later recovered his tortured body and, by good fortune, found his head in the bushes. They buried him at a place now called Bury St Edmunds. He was said to perform miracles and he was called a saint.

Once the Danes had collected all the treasures they could find and they were satisfied that the kingdom was fully subdued, Ivarr conferred with his brother Halfdan and the other leaders. He advised of his intent to go back to Northumbria before meeting up with Olafr the White to attack the kingdom of Strathclyde as had been agreed. Halfdan, always eager to carry on the fight, wanted to take the conquest from East Anglia and East Mercia into Wessex and was keen to lead his own army. Ivarr, who was wise in the way he achieved his objectives gave advice to Halfdan.

"I have informed you of my strategies and I have not been found wanting in my judgement. I now advise you strongly, having seen the men of Wessex at Nottingham and knowing of them from my campaigns into Kent, you should not take precipitous action in Wessex. Our army needs to be reinforced to give us superior numbers. Even then you should not be too hasty but take your time to wear down their resistance by superior strategy and intelligence."

Halfdan agreed that he would send for reinforcements by asking King Guthrum to bring his army from Denmark to assist in the conquest of Wessex. In the meantime, Halfdan remained at Thetford during the winter but took time to loot the towns of Ely, Ramsey and Crowland.

Ivarr returned to Northumbria and saw that Ubbe had been thorough in his defences and organisation. Sigurdr had earlier joined his brother Ubbe. He had come to advise of the events in Scotland and to relate Olafr's arrangements to co-ordinate events. During this time, Sigurdr and Ubbe had met the few surviving royal family of Deira, the southern part of the kingdom of Northumbria, who had submitted to the rule of the Danes under Ubbe. They had paid danegeld to limit the destruction of the kingdom and save their lives. They had no option but to cooperate and had accepted the Dane's appointment of Egberht for the time being as the tributary ruler of Northumbria.

During a meeting in King Osberht's Hall Sigurdr had noticed a Northumbrian princess called Blaeja. She was a vivacious woman who had thick red hair and who had shown more spirit than her younger brother when the Danes were discussing changes to the running of the kingdom. She wore a long sleeved blue dress that was close fitting and flowed down to her ankles and which also revealed a comely figure. The bottom of the dress was trimmed with a red hem.

Freyja the Goddess of Love worked on Sigurdr for the first time in his life and he became intrigued by Blaeja and, though she hid it well, Blaeja was also attracted to his manly physical presence. Blaeja's younger brother did his best to keep him away from her, frustrating Sigurdr's interest which swelled his determination to know her better and made him single-minded in the same way that he would pursue his quarry in battle. His unsubtle approach caused Blaeja to show some indifference that again put flame to the fire. The excuses of the brother eventually became explosive and Sigurdr threatened him with death if he continued to frustrate his wishes to talk to her. Blaeja was promptly presented to Sigurdr who, unused to such emotions over a woman, found the conversation difficult to start. Blaeja sensed his difficulties and opened the conversation with a direct question.

"Why have you summoned me to see you, am I to be your slave?"

"No," said Sigurdr, "I merely seek your company."

Blaeja replied, "In that case, why do you need to threaten the life of my brother? Is my presence so important that you would have my company only as a grieving sister?"

Sigurdr was chastened, and replied, "I do not want to see you grieving but I am unused to being frustrated in my actions by any man. I want us to get to know one another naturally and so we shall continue to meet without the controlling influence of your brother."

"Very well, but I will not be commanded, and shall only agree if it be by my own free will," said Blaeja. Sigurdr respected this and agreed it should be so.

At each meeting and over time Sigurdr and Blaeja grew to like each other better the more each knew about the other. Despite Sigurdr's lack of soft words and subtlety, Blaeja came to trust him, recognising he was true to himself and true to others. Blaeja, unusually for a Saxon princess, had learnt to ride and she would ride out from York with Sigurdr regularly through the surrounding countryside. Eventually on such a ride, among the meadows bedecked in wild flowers and the flight of bees and butterflies, she consented to become his Queen.

Ivarr, despite his relentless campaigns, had taken a Norse wife in the early days in Dublin in 856AD, called Thora, where she resided. Ivarr's eldest son at this time was just thirteen years of age, some three years younger than Olafr's son Eysteinn. History records Ivarr's son attacking Lismore in 883AD but he never succeeded his father as king of Dublin. Ivarr's union led to the founding of the kings of York dynasty. His grandson Ragnall became the king of Northumbria based at York, and Ragnall's brothers, Sigtryggr and Gothfrith, true to family tradition, carried on their warlike traditions. Gothfrith was still fighting in Ireland when he led an attack on Armagh in 921AD at Martinmass. He later succeeded Ragnall as king of Northumbria. All his grandsons were still committed Pagans until their deaths, Sigtryggr dying in 927AD, and Gothfrith in 934AD.

Ivarr had been able to bring his wife to Northumbria at this time and they spent the winter together in York. She fell in love with the stone walled city and buildings with its churches and industry and its Saxon culture. This compared favourably with the more rudimentary fortifications at Dublin comprising the earthen banks and wooden ramparts with a wooden quay. She therefore agreed with Ivarr that she should reside there, now that Northumbria had been pacified and secured by the Danes and her children joined her.

With the passing of winter in 870AD, Ivarr took his army to join up with Olafr at Dumbarton in the kingdom of Strathclyde. Ubbe went south to meet up with Halfdan in Mercia, to assist with his campaign in Wessex.

In view of Sigurdr's marriage, it was arranged that he should stay in Northumbria to keep the kingdom in order. In 872AD, Sigurdr dispensed with Egberht and Bishop Wulfhere, who were taken in by King Burgred of Mercia but Egberht was later killed as a traitor.

The next year, news came from Zealand which required the urgent action of Ragnar's sons to preserve their kingdom. In the same year news came of Ivarr's death in Dublin. With Halfdan fully occupied in his campaign in Wessex it was agreed that Sigurdr should be the one to return to run the kingdom. Before leaving with his new queen, he appointed Ricsige to rule Northumbria and brought back Bishop Wulfhere. On arriving at Zealand, Sigurdr found that his mother had died many years before, and though she knew of Ragnar's death she knew little of what her sons had been doing and did not know whether they were alive or dead. Blaeja gave birth to her first child, a son called Horda Knutr.

Chapter 8

OLAFR AND THE SCOTS

Olafr had sailed with Auisle and Sigurdr to meet Cinaed MacAlpin the king of the Scots at their kingdom of Dal Riada, a small kingdom squeezed between the Pictish kingdom to the north and east, the Strathclyde Britons to the south, and the Gaill Gaedhil to the west. The Gaill Gaedhil comprised the Norse settlers on the west coast and the Western Isles, with a mixture of Celts and Norse through intermarriage.

Auisle arranged the introduction of Olafr to King Cinaed MacAlpin, and it was evident that Auisle had some influence with the Scots. However, he had claimed that he was a king representing the Gaill Gaedhil, and this claim was shown to be untrue. Olafr met King MacAlpin with his brother Domnall and his sons Constantine and Aed and a feast was prepared that afternoon. The king, though frail and elderly, animatedly pursued an alliance with Olafr against the Picts who had killed his father and the Strathclyde Britons whose kingdom stretched up from Cumbria to the banks of the River Clyde, and whose centre was at the stronghold of Dumbarton Rock on the north bank of the Clyde. Olafr was aware that his son by Aud the Deep Minded, the daughter of Ketill Flat Nose, was active in the north, carving out a kingdom from the Picts in Caithness, Moray, Ross and Sutherland. His son's name was Thorstein the Red and he had married Thuridr, the Granddaughter of the Irish King Cerball of Ossory. King MacAlpin saw the Norse as the dominant and growing force in the land continuing to settle the west coast and feared for the long-term survival of his kingdom. Olafr was keen to help his son in the north by attacking the Pictish kingdom in its heartland. An alliance was thus forged, and King MacAlpin offered his daughter Maelmuire to Olafr as his wife, to which Olafr agreed, knowing to refuse another wife would have put distrust into the alliance. It was shortly after the meeting that King MacAlpin died and was succeeded by his son Constantine.

Olafr and Auisle in the early part of the year 866AD led their army to attack the Picts who they defeated, taking hostages back to their camp in Dal Riada, to ensure the payment of a yearly tribute. King Constantine was very pleased to see the devastation brought upon the Picts, but was equally wary of the foreign force within his kingdom, particularly of Auisle with his crude and un-diplomatic manner. Olafr and Auisle continued to campaign among the Picts in the following year, weakening the kingdom to the benefit of the Scots. Olafr had spent little time with his new wife Maelmuire leading to Auisle saying, "Now you are old, you show no interest in your wife. You should release her to me to take care of her wants." Olafr, long irritated by Auisle, exploded with anger at the impertinence and struck at him with his axe but Auisle was nimble and only received a glancing blow. Drawing his sword he was about to strike Olafr, when Sigurdr killed him with his axe.

Word came back from Dublin that in the absence of Ivarr and Olafr, Aed Findliath had broken his alliance and carried on a war against the Vikings to good effect. Also the fortification that Olafr had built at Clondalkin as an outpost some ten miles from Dublin near the River Liffey had been attacked and burnt down. Olafr was therefore obliged to take his army back to Dublin, from where he attacked Armagh to check Aed Finliath's ambitions. Armagh was celebrating the feast of their Saint Patrick and many pilgrims had arrived to join the celebrations. In consequence Olafr was able to capture a large number of people who he took as slaves. He then returned to Dal Riada in 869AD, where Olafr and Sigurdr planned an attack on the Strathclyde Britons at Dumbarton, a task that would not be easily won from such a strong fortification. Sigurdr left for Northumbria to coordinate logistics with his brother Ivarr, but Ivarr needed to spend time at York with Ubbe to satisfy himself that the newly acquired kingdom was being properly managed. He arranged to join Olafr the next year. Sigurdr, with time on his hands, had turned to romance with his new love, Blaeja.

In 870AD, Ivarr led his army north to meet up with Olafr, both agreeing that a direct attack on the stronghold of Dumbarton would be wasteful in men and resources. They decided to cut off all supplies to Dumbarton and to starve them into submission, which took four months to achieve. Once the Strathclyde Britons had surrendered, Dumbarton was sacked and burnt to the ground and its inhabitants taken prisoner as slaves and shipped back to Dublin to be traded. They returned with a fleet of over two hundred ships.

Back in Dublin, word came from Vestfold that Olafr was required to return home to secure his kingdom. In earlier years he had been forced to share his kingdom with his half brother Halfdan Svarti, Olafr having taken over the western half of the kingdom. However Halfdan Svarti had unexpectedly died as he was crossing a lake on his sledge, when the ice gave way and he was drowned. Cattle had been earlier branded on the ice, and the cattle dung had weakened the ice as it absorbed the sun's rays. With Halfdan Svarti's sons being young and Olafr away from his kingdom, his realm was under threat and he began losing territory, as tributary kings started to rebel.

Olafr sailed for Vestfold in a long ship of 32 oars, and 75 feet in length. Olafr in later years was incapacitated suffering from acute arthritis and gout and unable to walk and, on his death, he was given a ship burial befitting such a great warrior. He was buried in his ship at Geirstadir, along with many fine goods, boats, sacrificed horses, dogs and a peacock. The ship, now known as the Gokstad ship was discovered one thousand years after its burial, well preserved in the blue clay. His stepmother, Queen Asa, was buried in a ship at Oseberg. Halfdan Svarti's son was Harold Haarfagre who had succeeded him to rule over his share of the kingdom. He was so named because of his fine thick hair and hence given the nickname Lufa meaning thick hair. Harold Haarfagre was to win back territory and eventually united the whole of Norway under his rule.

> A branch of Odin's line, King Olafr
> Long the proud support of Norway's realm
> Ruled over the western ocean, both far and wide
> Then by gout he was cruelly oppressed
> In Vestfold, Olafr lay down to sleep his last
> A warrior king beneath the heavy earth
> Lies buried at Geirstadir, in a ship's mound

With Ivarr and Olafr departed, King Constantine's sons, always ready to benefit from the efforts of others, arranged the assassination of King Artgha of the Strathclyde Britons in 872AD. Moving into the vacuum left by the departing Vikings, the Scots gained control of the Picts, and agreed to Thorstein the Red taking the northern half of Pictland. However, once Olafr had departed for Vestfold they did not fear retribution and felt strong enough to ignore their alliance with Olafr. They therefore betrayed Thorstein to the Picts by planning that they should murder him at Caithness when attending a meeting they had arranged. The small Scottish kingdom then began to establish control over what is now the whole of Scotland including the Norse, the Picts and most of the Strathclyde Britons.

Ivarr, on Olafr's departure, was now the sole king of Dublin and ruler of the Norse and Danish settlers in Ireland. With increasing age, the wear of his vigorous life and effect of the wounds inflicted had begun to show and his restless nature was stilled. Apart from a plundering foray around Ireland, when he took along Olafr the White's son, Eysteinn, as a future king. He spent his remaining years in Dublin with his family. This unceasing warrior, wily enough to always avoid defeat in battle but who successfully conquered the kingdoms of Northumbria, East Mercia and East Anglia, died in his bed in his

Dublin kingdom in the year 873AD. The kingship of Dublin then passed to Olafr's son Eysteinn, who was the grandson of the High King Aed Findliath. Eysteinn was also married to the daughter of the Irish King Cerball of Ossory.

Chapter 9

OLAFR'S LINE IN AMERICA

On the news of Thorstein's death, his mother, Aud the Deep Minded, aware of the uncertain future developing with the expansion of the Scottish lands, decided to leave for Iceland to be with her brothers Bjorn and Helgi and her sister Thorunn. Her father Ketill Flat Nose had already died. In her weakened situation and fearful that to put consolidating wealth on board a ship would attract the interest of thieves and pirates, she secretly had Knorr ships built in the forest. The Knorr ship was wider and deeper than the Long Ship, being designed to more easily carry cargo and livestock.

Many of her kinsmen chose to follow Aud. Her sister Jorunn the Wise with her son Ketill, the Lucky Fisher, came along with such respected leaders as Koll, known as Dala-Koll. She took along her son Thorstein's children, sailing first to the Orkneys, where she arranged the marriage of her granddaughter Groa, to Jarl Thorfinn. From there, she sailed northwest to the Faroe Islands situated in the wild North Atlantic Ocean, half way towards Iceland. Here she arranged the marriage of a second granddaughter called Olof amongst the distinguished Gotuskeggi clan. Arriving in Iceland with her grandson Olafr Feilan and the younger unmarried sisters, Thorgerd, Osk, Vigdis and Thorhild, she met her brothers Helgi and Bjorn, and stayed the winter with Bjorn. The next summer she travelled to Laxerdal, where she founded her settlement and her farm called Hvamm with the help of Irish and Scottish slaves, who she later made free with gifts of land. A year after founding the farm, her granddaughter Thorgerd married Dala-Koll, and she gave her land where Koll set up a farm on the banks of the Laxa River. Aud also gave out further land to those who had accompanied her and so the settlement grew.

Nearing her death, Aud was secretive about her ailments and was sharp tongued to anyone who enquired about her struggles. She arranged the marriage of her grandson Olafr Feilan to Alfdis and a large reception was arranged for all her kinsmen. Aud most loved Olafr above all others, and announced at the reception that she was giving the farm of Hvamm to him and asked her brothers to be witness. That night she died in bed. Olafr found her the next day sitting upright on the pillows. In honour of her leadership and judgement, they raised a burial mound and buried her in a ship along with many valuable grave goods.

From the descendants of the union between Olafr the White and Aud, through their son Thorstein, one Thorfinn Karlsefni was recorded in the Icelandic Sagas, detailing his exploits in North America.

Eric the Red had established a colony in Greenland and had three sons, Thorstein, Leif the Lucky and Thorvald and an illegitimate daughter called Freydis. Leif the Lucky, on trading to Norway, had been instructed by the king to bring Christianity to Greenland and he was largely successful in this. His mother was converted to Christianity but Eric the Red was not. His mother then withdrew from Eric's bed, much to his disgust. Leif first came to know of the lands of North America to the southwest from Bjarni Herjolfsson, who had missed landfall off Greenland and found himself far to the south off the coast of North America. Bjarni had not explored the lands and it was left to Leif to make an expedition where he founded a camp by building long houses on the northeast point of the Newfoundland Island, named Leifsbudir.

Thorfinn Karlsefni was the son of Thord Horse Head and, on leaving Iceland, he had made himself wealthy trading to Norway and Ireland. He knew of the Greenland colony and decided to take a cargo of goods there, sailing with his friend Snorri Thorbrandson and forty men. He was made welcome by Eric the Red who traded for his goods, and invited him to stay the winter, which Thorfinn was pleased to accept. Staying with Eric the Red was his daughter in law, Gudrid Thorbjarnardottir, who was made a widow on the death of one of Eric's sons, Thorstein. She was the descendant of an Irish slave set free by Aud. Thorstein had set off on a voyage to Vinland in North America. However he became lost in the Atlantic, and spent the whole summer at sea before finding his way home where he died of a sickness.

During the long winter on Eric's farm, they played board games and told stories. Yule was particularly festive, with Thorfinn Karlsefni bringing out the malted barley from his ship's supplies to which was added water to make ale. Thorfinn began to take a growing interest in Gudrid that grew to the point where he asked her to marry him. She replied that she would defer to the wishes of Eric, who in the event agreed to the marriage, when further festivities took place. It was during this time that Thorfinn heard of Leif's travels to North America and of the cargoes of maple tree logs brought back with wine berries. Descriptions of the rivers teeming with salmon and the forests full of game whetted his appetite to know more. Following the marriage, he resolved to found a permanent settlement there with his new wife.

As summer came, the expedition was brought together with three ships provisioned for the voyage to take one hundred and forty men and five women, plus their livestock. Thorfinn Karlsefni with Snorri Thorbrandson commanded one ship on which Thorfinn's wife Gudrid also sailed. Bjarni Grimolfson commanded a second ship with Thorhall Gamlason, and forty men. Thorvard commanded the third ship, and he was the husband of Eric the Red's daughter, Freydis. She was a domineering and spiteful woman, married to a man for his wealth but who had few admirable features either in physical appearance or personality. Freydis, despite her bitter and nasty disposition was a determined and brave woman. Also on

Thorvard's ship was Eric the Red's son, Thorvald, and Thorhall the Huntsman. Thorhall was a man of coarse features with black hair that went with his ability to cause both trouble and insult in the manner of his speech, interspersed as it was with periods of long brooding silences, skulking away from the others. He was however very experienced in the exploration of North America from previous expeditions.

The ships sailed down the coast of Labrador, which had been named Helluland after the large stone slabs making up the shoreline. They then passed the forested areas named Markland, before arriving at an island just north of Leif's camp in Newfoundland. They saw a bear on the island and named it Bjarney - Bear Island. They did not stop at Leif's camp but sailed on into the Saint Lawrence Seaway to make landfall on the northeast cape of Nova Scotia named Kjalarness. This point was so named, since a ship on an earlier expedition had been grounded there by storms breaking the keel on the rocks. The crew had spent a long time replacing the keel and repairing the planking. Thorfinn found the old keel still there, before sailing south along the coast of Nova Scotia, which they named wonder beaches from the miles of white sand which never seemed to end. Rounding the southwest point of Nova Scotia, they explored the coastline of the mainland previously named by Leif as Vinland. Going into a fjord, with an island at the mouth, they encountered very strong currents, and so named the island Straumsey, and the bay, Straumsfjord. On the shoreline they found many bird's nests with eggs, which were so numerous it was difficult to walk without stepping on them. The grass growing naturally was good for use as pasture, and they disembarked the livestock and explored the land thereabout. They decided to settle here and during the early winter, Gudrid gave birth to Thorfinn's son, who they named Snorri after Thorfinn's friend Snorri Thorbrandson. The first Vinlander of European stock was thus directly descended from Aud the Deep Minded, and Olafr the White.

As winter drew on it became very severe. They had not properly prepared for their survival in such conditions and could find little food to sustain them in the bitter cold. Thorhall the Huntsman had complained about the situation and lack of foresight and planning, and he accused Thorfinn and Bjarni of being gormless, which in the Norse sense meant failing to take heed. He then went missing for three days. Thorfinn found him kneeling at the edge of a cliff, looking up to the heavens in a semi trance. As was his nature, he would say little of what he had been doing and saw no reason to confide in anyone. It then transpired that the men had come across a beached whale, and all went to cut the meat and boil it. Thorhall then said, "My poem to Old Red Beard asking for food was answered, which is more than your Christian God could deliver." Those who were Christians were unsure of taking food from Thor's table, Thor being the son of Odin the God of War. However those who had taken the food became ill with stomach complaints and they threw the meat away. The weather then eased and in the spring they made successful fishing expeditions, and found newly laid eggs.

Thorhall the Huntsman continued to complain about the leadership and wanted to explore the north, whilst the others wanted to explore the south. Eventually Thorhall persuaded nine men to go with him in one of the ships but bad storms took him out into the Atlantic, and they were never heard of again. Thorfinn Karlsefni and Snorri Thorbrandson sailed south along the coast of Vinland with forty men, leaving behind Gudrid in the care of Bjarni and the other men. They took some livestock with them and arrived near the Hudson River at an inlet they called Hop that meant a land locked bay since it was a tidal pool that dried out and the river could only be gained at high tide. The river was teeming with fish, and large herds of deer roamed round about, amongst the self-sown wheat and wild wine berries. Thorfinn and his men dug dykes at the high water mark and they were able to trap many flat fish as the tide went out.

After they had been there two weeks, nine hide-covered boats came down the river early in the morning. As the occupants landed on the shore they raised poles in the air and set them in a circular motion making a loud swishing noise. The men were short with black tangled hair, high cheekbones and had a wild threatening appearance. They then left as they had arrived.

Thorfinn spent the winter at Hop with his men, which was very mild and no snow fell throughout the period. In the spring a number of boats arrived with the intention of trading. They offered animal skins for the iron weapons but Thorfinn forbade his men from making such a dangerous trade. Instead they traded red cloth for the pelts, which the Indians wrapped around their heads and as the cloth started to run out, they accepted even thinly cut strips in exchange. The women brought out milk, which was equally popular, and they amassed a large number of animal skins in return. The bull that had been grazing among the trees, came out to see what the excited noises were about, and began bellowing loudly and aggressively. This frightened the Indians who tried to get inside the encampment, but Thorfinn's men defended the entrance to prevent this happening. One of the Indians tried to steal a sword and he was killed by one of Thorfinn's men. The Indians then withdrew in haste. Thorfinn expected trouble and strengthened the encampment with a palisade of wood.

Three weeks later a mass of boats came down the river, so thick that they looked like a vast swarm of black flies on the water. As they approached, they began waving their poles whilst screeching out their war cries. The Indian's main weapons were stones hurled from slings, and their bows with arrows tipped with stone arrowheads. They also had cumbersome stone axes. Thorfinn organised his men with their shields in a defensive shield wall and moved to engage the Indians as they tried to land. Thorfinn's men, through their discipline and superior weapons were able to kill many Indians with the loss of only one man, who fell from an arrow in the chest whilst still holding his axe. However they were heavily outnumbered, with Indians pouring out of the trees on their flanks, giving the impression that there was a second force. Thorfinn, not wanting to be outflanked with such large numbers of men, ordered his men to retreat to a cliff wall to better defend themselves. The Indians paused to look at the dead Viking, and picked up his axe and tried it out on a tree to good effect. They then tried it on a large stone, which broke the axe, causing them to conclude it was inferior to stone. They then threw it into the water.

As Thorfinn's men retreated past the encampment, a second man was killed when a heavy stone from a sling hit the back of his skull breaking it open. Eric the Red's daughter Freydis came out and berated the men for fleeing from such miserable opponents but they ignored her as they ran past. She began to follow the men but being heavily pregnant, she was very slow. Seeing the Indians coming towards her, she picked up the dead Viking's sword to defend herself. As they approached, she bared one breast from her bodice, and slapped it with the sword. The Indians at the forefront were taken aback to see a pregnant woman with hatred in her eyes showing no fear and ready to defend herself to the death. They broke away and those behind followed a hasty retreat to their boats, leaving their dead behind. Thorfinn and his men marvelled at the luck that had fallen to Freydis. Freydis could not be faulted for her courage but she was an evil and quarrelsome woman and, later, Sagas recorded her involvement in the murder of many of her compatriots including women. She had inherited her father's temperament for Eric the Red had been made an outlaw for murder, both in Norway and in Iceland and had to flee for his life as anyone then had the right to kill him. Many thought that Hel, the Goddess of the underworld that she ruled, would come and take Freydis to the place for the wicked, known as slaa ihjel, literally slain in hell.

Since Thorfinn and his men slept uneasily under the constant threat of a repeat attack, they decided to decamp and sail north. They discovered five Indians sleeping in skin sacks by the shore. They killed them suspecting they were outlaws and thus fair game under their Nordic laws. The Indians had vessels containing deer bone marrow blended with blood.

Arriving back at Straumsfjord, Thorfinn was eager to see Gudrid and his son Snorri. After a period with Gudrid, and hearing that Thorhall the Huntsman had not returned, he felt duty bound to sail north to look for him. He sailed deep into the Saint Lawrence Seaway and up the river, where they lay to on the southern shore off lands that looked very attractive for settlement. A one legged Indian had crept down to the shore and, catching them by surprise, shot an arrow into Eric the Red's son Thorvald. It had penetrated deep into his intestines and Thorvald knew it would be fatal. He made a joke of the wound, as was their way to scorn death and accept their fate. As he pulled out the arrow he said, "That was some fat paunch which swallowed up the arrow." Thorfinn's men hunted for the Indian but he was remarkably swift in his movements and they only caught fleeting glimpses of his escape. Thorvald asked to be buried where the land had seemed so inviting as he lay dying from the poisonous contents spilling out from his intestines. Only Leif the Lucky now remained alive of Eric's three sons. On the return home they saw what they believed to be the settlement of the one legged Indian but they kept clear to avoid any further danger.

Thorfinn and his men stayed a third winter at Straumsfjord but quarrels broke out between the men who had no wives and the atmosphere became tense. The two ship commanders, Thorfinn Karlsefni and Bjarni Grimolfsson discussed the situation and could see no way of resolving the problem. They surmised that with the large number of men needed to defend their camp against the Indians, the settlement was not sustainable with only five women and, in these circumstances, they decided it was best to return to Greenland.

Bjarni was the first to leave with his men and all went well until they entered the Greenland Straits when the ship began to take on water as it worked in a choppy seaway. Inspecting the planking it became evident that it had become infested with worms during its stay in Vinland and the wood was rotten. The boat being towed behind was hauled alongside the ship and as many men as possible got into the boat which was unaffected by worms as its bottom had been covered in a seal's blubber tar. Only half the ship's crew could safely get into the boat and it was decided to draw lots to see who would go in the boat and who would stay on the ship. Bjarni was one whose lot entitled him to go in the boat but a young Icelander who was not so fortunate asked, "Are you going to desert me now Bjarni?"

Bjarni replied, "It must be so, for we are hapless."

"That is not what you promised me when I left my father's house to follow you," replied the Icelander.

"What do you suggest," asked Bjarni.

"That we change places," said the Icelander.

Bjarni replied, "You put a high price on your life and fear to die but I will change places."

Despite the slur cast on the young Icelander for his fear of dying, he accepted the change.

Bjarni and the remaining crew on the ship said their farewells as the boat and ship drifted apart. Bjarni and his crew were never seen again, as the ship foundered and the icy waters sucked out their body heat and with it their lives, causing them to lapse into unconsciousness within minutes.

Thorfinn Karlsefni sailed for Greenland in the summer, his son Snorri now being three years old. From Greenland he sailed with his cargo of maple wood and animal skins to trade in Norway, obtaining a good price due to their novelty. He then settled back in Iceland with Gudrid and his son Snorri, to carry on a life of farming. From Thorfinn's descendants came many distinguished men including Bishops.

Chapter 10

THE INVASION OF WESSEX

Halfdan, eager to begin the conquest of Wessex, despite Ivarr's advice, did not wait for the arrival of King Guthrum from Denmark but marched into Wessex to the royal estate of Reading in January of 871AD. He followed the old track known as the Icknield Way from Thetford, along the Downs to cross the River Thames at the ford at Cookham. Here he met up with his fleet that had sailed up the Thames and, passing the fortified Saches Island at Cookham, spears were exchanged with those on board the ships and the West Saxons on the island.

Halfdan had been taught well by the expertise of Ivarr and selected a strategic position east of the town of Reading to set up camp by the River Thames flowing from the northwest to the east at a point where it is joined by the River Kennet flowing from the west. With both sides of the camp protected by the rivers and an eight hundred yard ditch dug across the third side connecting the two rivers, now known as Plummery ditch, it was a strong defensive position. The camp was fortified with earthen banks and a wooden palisade and the gates placed in such positions as to best allow a surprise counter attack. The camp was capable of being defended easily by only 600 men with others required to tend the ships.

Two of the Jarls had been sent out on an exploratory raiding party to supplement provisions and to take what plunder they could find. The Great Windsor forest stretched southwest from the town of Maidenhythe on the River Thames to Newbury on the River Kennet. The Jarls took their men along the north bank of the River Kennet until they came to Eaglefield. At this place the Danes encountered the men of Berkshire under Earldorman Aethelwulf. Both sides joined in battle and held their lines for a long time, before the Danes were put to flight. One of the Jarls was killed and a large part of the raiding party was slain. Events moved quickly, as King Aethelred of Wessex and his younger brother Alfred combined their forces to attack the stronghold at Reading. Cutting down those Danes found outside the stronghold, they fought their way to the gates, taking casualties from those on the fortifications. As they struggled forward, two gates were suddenly opened, and a strong force of Danes rushed forward to attack both flanks of the Saxons. Ealdorman Aethelwulf, the victor at Eaglefield, was killed outside the stronghold but his body was recovered for burial in his Mercian homeland at Derby, despite the West Saxons being forced to flee from the onslaught. The West Saxon army was scattered, and they retreated across the ford at Twyford.

Finn and Gunnr had made a pledge to fight close to one another and to protect each other as the need arose, and they saved each other's lives on more than one occasion. They were inside the fortification when the West Saxons had fought their way to the gate and, under the orders of their Jarl, had burst out onto the West Saxon's left flank, as others burst out of a gate on their right flank. The West Saxons were taken by surprise and many fell but they held firm until the Danes succeeded in getting behind them and panic set in. Finn and Gunnr were close to where Ealdorman Aethelwulf fell from a spear thrust into him at close quarters and where the fighting was most intense. Aethelwulf's retainers were seasoned fighters and they did not give ground easily. Finn took a heavy blow to his helmet from a sword that knocked him unconscious but Gunnr was able to move forward to prevent him being stabbed with the sword. Finn needed three days to recover from the blow as he suffered a mild concussion and blurred eyesight.

Finn joked to Gunnr on recovering, "The Saxon welted me in a way I will never forget. He was tall and strong and bested me by forcing his shield down on to me and once off balance he unexpectedly kicked away my leg, and struck at me as I fell. My lug is singing louder than my gob can sing these days."

Halfdan, fed by success, allowed his sense of invincibility and impatience to cloud his judgement and, ignoring the words of caution given by his brother Ivarr, he took his army out into the field to confront the West Saxons four days later. His aim was to defeat the West Saxon army and then provision his men. He marched at the crack of dawn from Reading north up the banks of the Thames heading towards the royal estates at Wallingford. On reaching Goring in late morning, the Danes became aware of the Saxons on Kingstanding Hill to the north. They had positioned themselves well on high ground, with the chance of retreat across the River Thames to the east via the ford at Moulsford or to the west down a road towards Lowbury Hill. Halfdan brought his army up the Icknield Way to the high ground on Moulsford Downs and to the south of Kingstanding Hill. A valley called Ashdown separated the two armies. Halfdan divided his forces into two, with a weaker force under the Jarls to the east nearer the River Thames with the stronger force to the west under the leadership of the kings. He was anxious to commence battle during the limited daylight of a January winter's day. The West Saxons, seeing the splitting of his army, also split their forces into two shield walls, one under Alfred and one under King Aethelred. King Aethelred was in no hurry to engage the enemy, being near to his home base and he stayed in his tent to pray. Alfred arrived first in good order and eager to engage the enemy. He saw the army under the Jarls moving down the hill towards the river in an attempt to outflank Alfred's forces. King Aethelred had stayed in his tent. Alfred alone made a quick decision to charge the Jarls' forces before they could outflank them. With a mighty roar which made the body tremble, the West Saxons on their home ground, filled with rage and determination, drove the Jarls' forces back up the hill, so that Halfdan's forces to the west were also in danger of being outflanked by Alfred's forces moving forward. Kind Aethelred, hearing the mighty roar outside, left his tent and brought his forces forward to see that Halfdan's shield wall was now in disarray and vulnerable to an attack on both fronts. He therefore led a charge of his forces down the hill, the momentum of which broke through Halfdan's shield wall, and caused a rout of his forces. King Baegseg was killed along with Sidroc, Osbjorn, Fraena and Harold. The main fighting was concentrated around a solitary thorn bush, but the Danes were pursued and killed over a wide area of Ashdown and beyond, as they struggled back to their base at Reading.

Finn and Gunnr had been under the command of the Jarls and so took the brunt of the West Saxon's attack. Never before had they been in such a desperate situation with their comrades falling about them bloodied and dying, falling back and hindering one another, whilst being attacked from the front and the flank. Finn still did not feel fully recovered from the blow he had taken. The two friends kept together as they retreated well behind Halfdan's forces led by the kings. Seeing King Aethelred's forces cutting into Halfdan's men and seeing the remaining forces of the Jarls retreating and being hunted by Alfred's men, they made a run for the River Thames intending to retrace their steps back to the encampment at Reading. However they were separated from their comrades and saw that the West Saxons were already at the river and ahead of them. They therefore headed away from the river to the west and were targeted by a group of West Saxons. Running for their lives with their heavy weapons, their mouths dry from fear and their strength ebbing away, they took refuge in a wood, hiding under the bracken on a bank by a stream. Downstream, some beavers had built a lodge and flooded the area, which prevented access from this direction. They could hear the West Saxons looking for them in the wood. They came very close several times. It was a mild and sunny day but twilight came early. Towards the close of the day they heard a shuffling noise coming towards them. Trying to control their urge to breath heavily, they clasped their weapons into their hands ready to fight. "Its Brokkr," Finn gasped in relief as a badger shuffled out onto the bank. They decided they would leave the wood when it was dark and so managed to get back safely to the encampment.

Halfdan was severely chastened to lose thousands of men in defeat including kings and reflected on Ivarr's words of advice. However his luck and his spirits rose as Guthrum arrived from Denmark with his army and bands led by Oscetel and Anwend who had attached their men to his army. This influx of fresh experienced fighting men changed the balance in the Dane's favour, with the West Saxons depleted by losses at Ashdown. The Danes marched south from Reading with confidence, setting up camp at the end of the day at Basing, a settlement half way towards Winchester from Reading. Here, the West Saxons led by King Aethelred and Alfred confronted the Danes. Both sides incurred heavy losses but it was the West Saxons who first broke away. The svinfylking flying wedge, known as the swine array, and led by the berserkrs and the wolf coats eventually broke down the Saxon lines and they retreated towards Newbury, leaving the Danes in possession of the battlefield. The Danes moved back to their base in Reading to prepare their ground and, after resting their forces, they went up the Thames to take Wallingford, which now lay undefended. By now it was March, and the Danes left Wallingford to begin their push deep into Wessex, moving southwest towards Salisbury. The West Saxons left Newbury moving 12 miles west to intercept the Danes and battle was joined at Meretun, now known as Marten. Again the fighting was fierce but the West Saxons left the Danes in possession of the battlefield having suffered heavy losses. Unable to match the stronger forces put against them they retreated towards Salisbury. During the battle, King Aethelred was taken ill, the strain of the encounters bearing down heavily on his shoulders. Within weeks he was dead and Alfred became King of Wessex at the age of twenty-three years because Aethelred's oldest son was still a child and unable to lead the kingdom. King Alfred had his brother's body carried in state and buried at Wimborne Minster.

Alfred, on returning to Salisbury, was soon in battle again at Wilton, a few miles west of Salisbury. Again the West Saxons were defeated and Alfred was forced to seek terms from Halfdan. Though Halfdan was in a strong position, he accepted the payment of danegeld, with a neutral area being established around the River Avon in Hampshire, flowing south from Salisbury to Christchurch at the sea. Halfdan took his army back to Reading, allowing King Alfred time to raise the danegeld. When payment had been received, the Danes moved into Mercia in the autumn and established themselves in London, extracting further danegeld from King Burgred. Halfdan then took his army north into East Mercia, and established a winter camp at Torksey in Lincolnshire, situated on the River Trent where it meets the Roman canal known as the Fosse Dyke linking the River Trent to the River Witham at Lincoln. At this time the Danish writ covered Northumbria, East Mercia, East Anglia and the eastern half of Wessex from Kent to the River Avon.

In the spring of 873AD, the Danes sailed upstream on the River Trent past Nottingham and Burton, until they came to Repton. Here they established a winter fortification around a church, alongside the River Trent on one side, and which had a dyke dug around the other sides connecting into the River Trent. Halfdan's intent was to consolidate his grip on Mercia and in that winter he clashed with the forces of King Burgred. Two hundred and fifty Mercians were killed and buried in a sunken two-room building nearby, and many of the bodies were mutilated and their testicles cut off and replaced with Thor's hammer and a boar's tusk. One of the dead was a man nine feet tall. The Danes raised mounds for their dead and cremated some on the hill nearby. King Burgred, having reigned for twenty-two years, lost the will to resist and was forced to flee to Rome. The Danes set up a puppet ruler called Ceowulf over the Mercians, who the Saxons called the foolish king's Thegn. Even the Danes called him a gawk. Ceowulf was obliged to give hostages, promising to obey the instructions of the Danes to relinquish his power peacefully when they should request it and provide support to their operations. He was eventually deprived of his position and killed.

Halfdan had heard of his brother Ivarr's death in Dublin and, with the loss of two undisputed joint kings of great stature, representing both the interests of the Danes and the Norse, conflict arose when the Norse established Olafr the White's son Eysteinn as Ivarr's successor. The Danes perceived an advantage to the Norse and were concerned about Eysteinn's connection to the Irish. Halfdan was also aware that the Northumbrians had revolted against the puppet ruler Egberht. It was therefore agreed that Halfdan's army would split from that of Guthrum, Oscetel and Anwend and go back to Northumbria, whilst Guthrum's forces would continue their campaign in Wessex. It was also agreed that once Halfdan had secured his interests in Dublin, he and Ubbe would bring a fleet from Dublin to the Bristol Channel, and open up a second front in Wessex in the west.

Finn and Gunnr did not choose to follow Halfdan into Northumbria. With their Jarl dead, they had risen to be experienced commanders. They decided they would take their share of estate lands in East Mercia. Their experiences had been many covering Scotland, Ireland, England and France, and it was time to tell their stories to their children and their grandchildren. They had been lucky to survive the years of warfare, still physically whole and active. Gunnr took lands in south Lincolnshire, crossing the Wapontak of Wingeirbrigr – the bridge of the friendly spear, a crossing point over the River Witham south of Grantham. He established the settlement of Gonerby on land north of Grantham, and took up farming with a young Danish wife. Finn took lands in north Lincolnshire at Alkborough overlooking the wide estuary and confluence of the Rivers Humber and Trent, near the place he had once crossed with his horse into Northumbria. He was more interested in ships than farms and so bought a Knorr trading ship, intending to trade between York, the Norse and the Danes, as well as Dublin. It was during a stay at York, haggling for goods manufactured by the Danes in York, that he met and married a Norse girl, who gave him many children. He was a successful trader and became very wealthy.

Winter over, Halfdan and his brother Ubbe went back to Northumbria in the spring of 874AD, basing himself at York to raise an army to recover his brother's kingdom at Dublin. The expulsion and death of the tributary King Egberht, was rectified by his replacement, Ricsige, and the reinstatement of Bishop Wulfhere.

By this time the Danes had begun colonising Northumbria and East Mercia, setting up the Wapontaks which defined the administrative areas, within which was a prominent meeting place where disputes were settled and where weapons were kept outside the court enclosure. Both Lincolnshire and Yorkshire were divided up into three districts known as Ridings. Wives and families were being brought over from Denmark to join the Viking men as land was allocated. The crew of a Viking Long Ship would be given land, being known by the Danes as the summer seamen – Summer lede – villages such as Summerledeby would be founded, later corrupted by the English to Summerby. Many settlements took the name of the Viking Chief or the name of the farm. Land was strictly apportioned between those areas assigned to the English and those estate lands assigned to the Danes. In East Mercia, the five Danish boroughs were established, being Stamford, Leicester, Nottingham, Derby and Lincoln, accessed by the River Trent flowing from the area of Derby, north through Nottingham, and connected to Lincoln by canal before emptying into the wide mouth of the River Humber, or by the Viking Way, a trail leading south from the River Humber through Lincolnshire to Oakham. In Leicester, Ubbe's landing had been marked by a stone, known as Ubbestone but which the English changed to Humberstone.

Having fought many battles over ten years, and endured many privations, the Danes now wanted to enjoy their gains and settle down to farming their lands. Halfdan, with his relentless thirst for battle, bullied and hectored the settlers and became so unpopular that he was close to being driven out of Northumbria. Getting older and more impatient as he faced a further fight to retain the kingdom so dearly won with the death of his father Ragnar, he now appeared to the Nothumbrian Danes as unstable and they branded him as fey, a doomed man who it would be unsafe to follow. Raising what army he could, Halfdan first had to reopen the trading route from York to Dublin, which involved ships being taken into the River Forth from the North Sea and then being manhandled over land to the River Clyde, from which access to the Irish Sea was gained. He marched north to set up his camp at the mouth of the River Tyne, where his ships sailed up to join him. He first ravaged the northern kingdom of Northumbria known as Bernicia to inhibit the unrest shown towards the tributary King Egberht, which territory had so far been spared the plundering of the southern kingdom. The monks on the island of Lindisfarne, fearing an attack on the monastery, began wandering to seek a safe place for Saint Cuthbert's bones, and set up a new monastery. It was many decades later that they settled on an island on the River Tyne at Durham. They had contemplated going to Ireland during their journeys. At the same time the relics of Saint Columba were removed to Ireland from Dunkeld in Scotland and from Iona to avoid the threat from Halfdan's activities.

Halfdan attacked the Picts north of the River Forth then, following in Ivarr's footsteps, he hauled his ships twenty miles overland from the River Forth to the River Clyde, going on to attack the Strathclyde Britons at their stronghold of Dumbarton on the River Clyde, thus ensuring the river passage remained open to him. The Strathclyde

Britons had been severely weakened by the attacks from Ivarr and Olafr, and from the scheming of the Scots in the kingdom of Dal Riada. From the River Clyde he sailed for Dublin, intent on restoring the kingdom to the Danes. Halfdan's plan was to kill King Eysteinn and become king of Dublin but he did not have a strong enough force to challenge King Eysteinn and the Norse directly. As was normal amongst the Norse, on Olafr's return to Vestfold, he had left his son in the care of a foster father, a Norseman called Bardr, who had taken King Eysteinn on campaigns in Ireland and tutored him well.

Halfdan bided his time, awaiting a chance to find King Eysteinn alone. His Danish spies recorded King Eysteinn's movements and habits and the strength of his retainers about him. Halfdan bribed a Dane living at the king's hall and, at the dead of night, he and some of his men were led to where the king was sleeping. There he was murdered and Halfdan quickly called on the Danes to support him and declared himself king of Dublin before the Norse could react.

However the success was short lived because the Norse had invited Aed Findliath, the High King of the Irish, to a feast in Dublin. He used the occasion to attack Halfdan and his men to avenge the murder of his Grandson, supported as he was by the Norse. Halfdan was outnumbered and driven out of Dublin. He returned to Northumbria to recruit more forces to ensure he became king and the Danes retained their interests in Dublin. Again, his Northumbrian subjects deserted him, wanting no part in his ambition. Halfdan, unused to being thwarted in his campaigns, showed further signs of mental instability and his rages further alienated his subjects from him so that he was driven out. In the end he could only return to Ireland with three ships, which he took into Strangford Lough to prepare his ground. However Bardr, now proclaimed the Norse king of Dublin had been forewarned of his coming and his fleet trapped Halfdan's escape from the loch. The fight that followed led to

Halfdan's death, being outnumbered as he was but Bardr was left permanently lame.

So ended the life of a tireless warrior-king who, though defeated at times and lacking the cunning of his brother Ivarr, had an iron resolve and a boundless energy to achieve his goals. It was that will and determination to overcome all obstacles, allied with impatience in later life, which caused him to put aside caution and which led directly to his death in the Viking manner.

Ubbe heard of the death of Halfdan when he was campaigning in North Wales, having invaded with his fleet, forcing King Ruaidhri – Rodrick Mawr, to flee to Ireland. It was also at this time that Guthrum had sent his messengers from West Mercia, asking Ubbe to begin opening the second front on Wessex from the Bristol Channel, needing the combined fleet of Ubbe and Halfdan to penetrate the marshy retreats of the remaining West Saxons, and to stop the irritant of hit and run attacks on his forces. Guthrum was unaware of Halfdan's death and his expulsion from Northumbria and had been expecting his support to arrive with a substantial fleet.

Chapter 11

THE CONQUEST OF WESSEX

Guthrum, on parting from Halfdan's forces at Repton, moved into East Anglia to winter at Cambridge, staying there for a year. The Great army of Danes was now considerably reduced from the forces which Ivarr and his brothers commanded, due not only to the fragmentation of the forces, but also from losses in battle. King Alfred had not been idle, and had built up a fleet to counter the sea borne advantage of the Danes. In 875AD he had challenged a fleet of seven Long Ships, capturing one and putting the others to flight. Under the treaty with Guthrum, King Alfred still had the men of Wiltshire west of the River Avon, and the men of the shires still remained available to him being the uncommitted forces of Dorset, Devon and Somerset.

Guthrum with the other kings, Oscetel and Anwend, were bent on total conquest. Ignoring their treaty, they planned their campaign well in order to catch King Alfred by surprise. Their strategy was to establish a strong base on the south coast to bring the men of Dorset, Devon and Somerset into the field and defeat them, and so conquer the western part of Wessex to join the eastern part already taken under tribute. They decided on taking Wareham, ten miles south of Wimborne Minster, a strongly fortified town between the River Frome and the North River also called the Trent. These rivers flowed into Poole Harbour nearby, a well-sheltered natural harbour for Guthrum's Long Ships to anchor. To ensure surprise, the Field Division marched down to London in Mercian territory, crossing the Thames at Staines, before proceeding southwest to Wareham. They marched only at night, camping in secluded places by day, and made great speed to arrive at Wareham after 4 days marching. They were undetected by King Alfred's men and quickly took Wareham due to the element of surprise. At the same time, the main body went by sea, aiming to arrive at Poole Harbour simultaneously with the Field Division. They beached their ships on Brownsea Island situated in Poole harbour when they arrived.

King Alfred's army was already in the field, and quickly arrived outside Wareham. The walled town was protected on the north and south side by the two rivers, whilst the east side faced Poole Harbour. The only possible means of attack was from the west across gently rising land. Within the town walls were a nunnery, a farm and a priory. King Alfred blockaded the western approaches, but thought better of making an assault on such large fortified forces, noting the number of long ships in the harbour exceeding well over one hundred ships. He therefore decided to open negotiations. This took two months before it was agreed that they would leave the kingdom on payment of danegeld. The Danes swore oaths on Thor's ring and on the Christians' holy relics. Hostages were exchanged, with King Alfred being free to pick his own hostages of men close to King Guthrum.

Guthrum however had no intention of honouring the agreement. After receiving the danegeld from King Alfred he murdered the West Saxon hostages he had been given. The Field Division then broke out of the town, riding quickly on horses to Exeter. King Alfred, angered by his inability to prevent the break out, also pursued them on horses but was unable to catch them before they had taken Exeter. Guthrum was unconcerned about the inevitable fate of the Danish hostages held by King Alfred, who were put to death.

The Danish fleet put to sea with the larger forces but fog hampered their progress out of Poole Harbour. A wind sprang up, blowing away the fog, and they then proceeded south by Swanage to round the south eastern head of the Isle of Purbeck They struggled against a rising wind from the south west and, unable to use their sails, made heavy weather rowing westwards. The wind backed to the south quickly strengthening to storm force and, suddenly, the ships were in serious trouble. The oarsmen began to tire as the ships were blown towards the south coast of the Isle of Purbeck, the seas throwing the ships in all directions. Some of the ships became rudderless, as the steering oars broke from the pressure of water moving against them, and some twisted in the heavy seas, breaking the mast stays, bringing the masts down onto the seamen. Many were cast over the side, and drowned in their heavy armour. Those still in the ships being repeatedly thrown down on to the shore by the heavy seas until all was broken apart, were too exhausted to save themselves from the boiling cauldron around them. The West Saxons killed those few men who made it ashore. In all over three thousand men perished with the loss of one hundred and twenty ships. The West Saxons saw it as the hand of God, punishing the Danes for breaking their oaths on the holy relics. Guthrum's forces were now weakened without ships to penetrate the rivers and were totally reliant on Ubbe and Halfdan joining them with their ships in the west.

King Guthrum thus went from a strong position to one that was hopeless. He agreed to leave Wessex in the autumn, giving hostages and swearing on oaths to fulfil his promises. As agreed, he marched his army from Exeter north into West Mercia and established his camp at Gloucester on the River Severn. Alfred meanwhile had taken his army to the royal estate of Chippenham, some thirty miles to the south of Gloucester. In happier times, his sister Aethelswith had married King Burgred of Mercia at the estate.

At Gloucester, King Guthrum had been able to bring in reinforcements as winter approached, and planned to capture King Alfred with a surprise attack on Chippenham. On January 6th 878AD, whilst the West Saxons were still celebrating Christmas and, with the town lightly garrisoned, Guthrum took Chippenham opposed only by a token resistance, and the West Saxons submitted. Alfred with a few of his men and his family had been able to flee into the marshes of

Somerset, looking for food and shelter. The whole of England now lay in the hands of the Danes, from Northumbria south into East and West Mercia, into East Anglia and now finally the submission of the West Saxons in Wessex.

Alfred's position now seemed hopeless but his dogged belief in his Christian God and a moral sense driving him on to do what was right until the end, kept his spirit uncrushed. He was pursued by the Danes on horseback, and was saddened to find that his fellow countrymen had turned against him, offering little help, shelter or food. Such was human weakness to turn on those whose fortunes were down and defenceless. There were those who were informing against their own king. Many reneged on their vows of loyalty to the king, and defected to the Danes. Ealdorman Wulfhere of Wiltshire being one who deserted the king and allied with the Danes.

King Alfred and his band of men had been forced to fight, to borrow and to steal in order to survive. After several weeks in the marshes King Alfred had stayed at a small cottage and here John the monk gave him help and assistance. King Alfred later made John the monk an abbot. King Alfred prayed to thank God for his escape, then saying, "Dear Lord, give me the strength, courage and wisdom in leadership to prevent our Christian kingdom being consumed by the Pagan Danes and the loss of all that is so dear to us. Bring back those of my subjects who have deserted me and give them faith again in thy works. Dear Lord show me the way that I may further thy will, for the sake of thy son Jesus Christ." As he fell into an exhausted sleep, Saint Cuthbert appeared to him in a vivid dream, speaking to him and giving him heart and guidance on what he now had to do.

King Alfred's first priority had been to establish a safe fortification to house his few retainers and family, which included his son Prince Edward and his daughter Aelfthryth. Alfred found his base nearby on the island of Athelney, or island of the Princes, which he then fortified. It had been the home of the hermit Saint Ethelwin and was surrounded by impenetrable marshes thick with vegetation and sinking underfoot. It lay on the River Tone, a small tributary of the River Parrett that flowed north into the Bristol Channel. When completed it was accessed by a causeway coming from the direction of East Lyng, the causeway ending at a deep ditch crossed by a removable wooden bridge. The ditch went all round the island bordered by a steep bank onto the island. On the island itself was a double wooden palisade. Any attacker getting over the first barrier would then have to drop twenty feet into a confined pit exposed to the arrows and spears of the Saxons or be perched on the first barrier struggling to get a ladder over it and hence equally vulnerable. The first barrier also obstructed the view of attacking archers to target the Saxons behind the second barrier. In the centre was a church built in 700AD, later made into a monastery at which John the monk became the abbot. From this base, King Alfred, with the few remaining warriors, was able to organise damaging raids on the Danes now more scattered in Wessex, and also able to keep in touch with the still loyal men of Wiltshire and Hampshire. The young Prince Edward would see his father praying before leaving with his men to carry out raids and to meet up with his loyal subjects. Alfred's family in this time of uncertainty were relieved every time he returned safely to the fortification, and this hardened Prince Edward to become the warrior he grew into, earning the title of Ironside. His daughter Aelfthryth also became a great campaigner, spending more time in the saddle than with her husband.

King Alfred was aware that any threat to his base was more likely to come from the sea via the River Parrett. He instructed the men of Devonshire to man defences at Cannington Hill Fort just to the south of Combwich. This was a settlement on the west bank of the River Parrett near its mouth.

King Guthrum was stung by the irritating raids by King Alfred's men in the marshes, launched from a strong defensive fortification on Guthrum's now more scattered forces, and his ability to bring together those still able to resist the Danes. He sent word to Ubbe asking him to open a flank from the sea into north Devon with his brother Halfdan, unaware that Halfdan was dead and his small fleet captured. Ubbe moved a fleet of twenty-three ships into the Bristol Channel and, on instructions from King Guthrum, moved his fleet into the River Parrett. Ubbe, seeing the fortification which was manned by Ealdorman Odda with the Devonshire army, landed his men ashore and chose to blockade it, knowing that they had few provisions and no access to water and had poor defences. Ealdorman Odda and the men of Devon realised that they would be weakened with time, and would face ultimate defeat, so they decided to act whilst they still had the strength and the will to fight. Waiting until first light, their bodies tense with fear and excitement, Odda and his men burst forth in desperation from the fort to attack the Danes. Ubbe and his men were caught unawares, heavily asleep, and some without their armour, and all without the protection of a shield wall. Only a few escaped back to the ships, and Ubbe was one of those killed. The Raven Banner woven by his sisters and endowed with magic powers to ensure victory, fell into the hands of the West Saxons to their great delight. The ravens represented those of Odin, Huggin and Muninn, - thought and memory.

Ubbe was the last of Ragnar's sons to die in the field of battle. Just three sons had survived to die a natural death, Ivarr in Dublin, Bjorn Ironside still living on his estates in France, whilst Sigurdr Snake in the Eye had taken his Northumbrian bride back to Zealand to reclaim his father's kingdom.

King Alfred's resolve stiffened against his Pagan enemy, as the men of Somerset were ready to join him. He now knew that a second front would not open behind him. It was now Easter and the king's Reeve went to the Folk Moots to call out the men in the shires to meet at the boundary marker of Egbert's stone, east of Selwood, and which is now called Kingston Deverill. It was seven weeks later that the meeting took place, as King Alfred rode to the Mark in Wiltshire. The men of Somerset, Wiltshire and those of Hampshire to the west of the River Avon greeted him warmly. A great cheer went up by those gathered at the stone ready to fight, expressing their joy on seeing King Alfred alive and there to lead them. By this time King Alfred was an experienced commander of his forces, having been battle hardened by his many encounters with the Danes. He knew how to best deploy and use his forces. Seeing that his men were eager and ready for battle. He marched north to Iley Oak near Crockerton, where he camped for the night. At dawn he again marched north towards Edington on the edge of Salisbury Plain.

Guthrum had been alerted to the rallying of the West Saxons, as villages emptied and spies informed of King Alfred's movements. Guthrum had brought his forces down the Ridgeway and camped on higher ground at the iron age Hill Fort of Bratton Camp, just to the south of Edington. King Guthrum, without the long experience and advice of Ivarr and Halfdan amongst his army, had neglected the Danes tradition of holding a strong fortification. Chippenham was not further fortified, nor was a fall back defensive position created in the event of retreat.

King Alfred decided not to attempt to scale the sheer sides of Bratton Camp. Instead he tried to entice Guthrum to engage him in battle. Guthrum had the stronger force, swelled by disloyal West Saxons, whilst King Alfred, unlike Guthrum, had no mounted warriors, and so Guthrum chose to meet Alfred in battle confident of victory.

The two sides formed their overlapping shield walls and moved towards one another, the West Saxons making their traditional chants of oot, oot, oot, whilst banging their weapons on their shields in time to their chants to give added effect. Both sides held firm for a long time, but slowly a part of the Dane's shield wall began to collapse at one end, and the West Saxons were able to get behind the defensive wall, which began to cause panic amongst the Danes, who eventually began to flee. A great slaughter took place as the West Saxons chased the Danes the fifteen miles back to their stronghold at Chippenham. The West Saxons on arriving at Chippenham, killed all Danes outside the stronghold, took away all the livestock they could find and began a blockade to starve them out. After two weeks, the Danes became desperate from hunger and began to despair of their hopeless situation. Guthrum knew that having once lost their kingdom, the West Saxons would give no quarter until the Danes were defeated. He could see that they were determined to maintain the siege until total surrender and so sought to negotiate as best as he could. Having reneged on his agreements before, Guthrum could see no possibility of escape this time and so he sent an emissary to King Alfred to seek peace.

The emissary began, "My Lord King Guthrum seeks a permanent peace between us, and asks your indulgence for the bad faith and treachery he has shown towards you and for which he now seeks to give redress. He offers to leave your kingdom and to give hostages of your choosing to ensure he honours his words and oaths. He seeks no hostages from you, finding his army sorely depleted and in distressed circumstances. The Saxons in their ancestral homeland have always been allies of the Danes, and King Guthrum's wish is to now live at peace with the West Saxons of Wessex and to be agreed by treaty".

The entreaty softened King Alfred's heart towards Guthrum and he replied to Guthrum's emissary.

"Tell your Lord my terms. I shall allow him to leave Wessex without his plunder and the gold and silver paid to him and I shall choose many hostages so that your king will suffer greatly at their loss, should his words be false. It is my condition that King Guthrum becomes a Christian and that he shall return to Wessex to be baptised along with the other kings and chiefs. The kingdom of Wessex shall incorporate the lands of West Mercia, so that the Dane Law shall run north of this mark, which we will define by treaty. King Guthrum and your leaders, before departing, shall swear an oath on our Christian relics and on Thor's ring that they will honour this agreement."

King Guthrum and the surviving Danish leaders met King Alfred to conclude the agreement which defined the boundary with the Dane Law necessary to establish a permanent peace. The Dane Law, incorporating East Mercia, East Anglia and Northumbria was situated north of a line that ran from the River Thames at London up the River Lea to its source, then in a straight line to Bedford, up the River Ouse to Watling Street, before terminating in the Wirral at Chester. King Guthrum thus controlled the north bank of the Thames to London.

King Alfred chose many hostages including those to be baptised and the arrangements for the baptisms were made at a church near Egbert's Stone at Aller. Oaths were sworn and then King Guthrum left in peace.

Several weeks later he returned with 30 of his followers to be baptised at Aller. They were clothed in white gowns for the ceremony. King Alfred raised Guthrum up from the stone font to receive him as his adopted son, giving him the name of Athelstan. The ceremony over, the celebrations began at the royal manor at Wedmore and went on for several days. King Alfred gave presents to the baptised Danes who stayed in Wessex until the autumn before returning to East Anglia.

On the departure of the Danes, King Alfred set about restoring his kingdom. He was guided by his Christian teachings and thankful to

God for the deliverance of his kingdom. He was merciful and did not have Ealdorman Wulfhere of Wiltshire killed for deserting his king, a serious crime in Saxon eyes but, instead, he had his lands and property confiscated.

King Guthrum honoured his agreement, though he took part in raids on France, and aided Vikings operating on the English coast. He ruled as a Christian Danish king of East Anglia, who minted his coins in London under the name Athelstan and who died in 890AD. King Alfred died in 899AD at the age of fifty, plagued with ill health throughout his life and worn down by the physical demands required of him as a Christian king in troubled times.

The mercy shown by King Alfred, after Guthrum's treachery and many betrayals, Alfred's humanity and humility exercised without weakness and his Christian values had worked their miracle on Guthrum. In time the Danes came to honour King Edmund of East Anglia as a true saint, martyred by Ivarr. And so, after nearly a hundred years, the burning hatred of the Danes for the Christian king, Charles the Great, who threatened their sovereignty and their religion, who removed their Saxon allies from their homelands converting them at the point of a spear, cutting down their sacred trees, this hatred had finally been spent. Conquest and colonisation saw the Danes adopt Christianity after ravaging Europe and causing so much misery, death and destruction, to the Christian communities. Whilst a Danish king subsequently came to rule all England again by conquest, King Knut, (Canute), was a Christian king who ruled wisely. King Knut, kneeling before the tomb of Saint Edmund, took his crown from his head, and laid it on the shrine to the martyr. It was later in 1066AD that the descendants of the Vikings who had settled in Normandy under Rolf the Ganger, came back to conquer England under the leadership of King William the Conqueror and to build their Norman castles and the churches and cathedrals that we see today.

Of those Vikings; whose vitality, courage and skills in seamanship and the arts of war had brought about the conquest of kingdoms; few could equal the achievements of Ragnar Lothbrok and his sons, and the magnitude of the effect they had on the history of the British Isles and Ireland.

Chapter 12

THE DECLINE OF THE HOLY ROMAN EMPIRE

AND EVENTS IN DENMARK

This book would not be complete without telling the wider story of the decline of the Holy Roman Empire. Whilst Ragnar and his sons had great influence on England, Scotland and Ireland, and Bjorn Ironside left his mark in Francia and the Mediterranean, Christian Europe came very close to seeing the Danes and Norse become their masters. Some seventy years earlier, the Danish King Gothfrith had threatened to take the fight to the gates of Charles the Great's palace at Aix-la-Chapelle (Aachen), before he was assassinated. This threat was belatedly fulfilled when the Danes stabled their horses in the aisles of his churches and burnt down his palace.

Charles the Great died in 814AD and was succeeded by his son Lewis the Pious who had three sons by his wife Irmingard. The eldest was Lothair, the second son was Pippin, and the third son Lewis the German. Lewis the Pious had sought an ordered progression by naming Lothair as his heir to the empire, with Pippin ruling Aquitaine and Lewis the German ruling Bavaria, both as under kings to Lothair. Lothair was later given the kingdom of Italy to rule under his father. Destiny decreed otherwise. Irmingard became ill and died in 818AD, which caused Lewis the Pious to lapse into great melancholy. He was urged to remarry, and took as his wife, Judith, the beautiful daughter of the Bavarian-Swiss Count Welf of Altdorf and his Saxon wife. From the seeds of this marriage, Charles the Great's vast empire, built on so much blood, was soon to weaken and fragment into civil war.

The Danish kingdom had been similarly weakened when, in 810AD, King Gothfrith was assassinated on the banks of the River Elbe after leading his army into Saxony to attack the Franks. His nephew Hemming, who led the army back into Denmark, died two years later, and the Danish kingdom was thrown into disarray. A power struggle developed between Gothfith's nephew Sigfrid and the nephew of an earlier king called Anulo. Both died in the struggle. The brothers of Anulo's nephew were Haraldr and Reginfrid, who then seized power as joint kings. Gothfith's sons, Horic and his younger brother took refuge in Sweden. Haraldr, acutely aware of his vulnerability, sought peace and support from the emperor, Lewis the Pious, an act that caused suspicion and loss of support among the Danes. However, Horic and his younger brother returned from their exile and, with the help of the disaffected Danes, killed Reginfrid, causing Haraldr to flee to the court of Lewis the Pious. Haraldr sought support to regain power, and, four years later in 819AD, with the forces of Lewis the Pious and the Danes' natural enemies, the Abodrites, he returned to Denmark. An uneasy peace was agreed between Haraldr, Horic and his brother, ruling as three separate kings. The Danes' distrust of Haraldr was increased, when in 826AD, he and his wife went to the court of Lewis the Pious at Ingelheim to be baptised, with Lewis the Pious and the empress Judith, standing as Godparents. As a reward he was granted lands in Frisia. He returned to Denmark with Saint Anskar under his protection, a Saxon orphan brought up by the clergy, who was to convert the Danes. A school was to be set up in Holstein, Anskar having brought with him Danish boy slaves purchased from the Christians, to be raised by the church as missionaries. Within a year Horic and his brother, supported by the Danes' distrust of any foreign influences, forced Haraldr to flee into exile in Frisia. Anskar also fled, but returned in 849AD to commence a second mission. Horic was then sole king and, after much persuasion, allowed a church in Schleswig and, consequently, the beginning of a long conversion of the Danes.

Whilst the Danish Kingdom had been engaged in internal turmoil, during this period the Jarls and leaders of the war bands, following the flight of King Haraldr, had organised their shipping exploits to great effect. Taking advantage of the civil wars and divisions in the Holy Roman Empire, they began to ravage it at large. In 837AD they had captured Walcheren, and soon Frisia was a base for their raids further a-field.

The disintegration of the empire had begun in 830AD. The second wife of Lewis the Pious had given birth to a daughter followed by a son Charles, later known as Charles the Bald. The scheming of his mother, Judith, and the indulgence of Lewis the Pious towards his young son and wife bred the conditions for resentment and distrust. Lewis the Pious assigned Alamannia to young Charles, under Count Bernard as Regent, causing Lothair to march his army from Italy, to be joined by Pippin from Aquitaine. On their arrival in Paris, Judith was taken and forced into a convent, Count Bernard was accused of adultery with Judith before he fled, and Charles then ten years of age was put in prison. Lewis the German meanwhile had attacked Alamannia.

Lewis the Pious had been campaigning away elsewhere, but by the summer of 833AD his army was facing those of his sons, between Basle and Strasburg. However his soldiers continued to desert him and he was eventually forced to give way. He was then humiliated by being dragged behind the carriage of his son.

The civil war was not however to end there. In 834AD, Pippin with Lewis the German restored their father to power after deposing Lothair who retired to Italy. Lewis the Pious was prevented from pursuing Lothair into Italy as the Danes were harrying Frisia and plundering and burning Dorstad. He was however unable to curb his favouritism for Charles, granting him a part of Neustria, causing Lewis the German to revolt. However he was not supported by

Pippin and had to give way, losing Saxony to Charles, who was also given the best part of Francia. Pippin died soon afterwards, leaving a young son aged sixteen, also called Pippin. He was seen as a natural king, fearless and brave, having the full support of the Aquitanians. Lewis the German was again forced into revolt, when his father refused to ratify the young Pippin as king, giving Aquitaine to Charles. Judith, recognising the failing health of Lewis the Pious from consumption, decided that she had to split the loyalties of the brothers, and instigated an alliance with Lothair in 839AD. Lothair's territory was fixed as Italy, an imperial title for Provence, the larger part of Germany, plus Frisia and Belgium. Charles was to hold Aquitaine and Neustria. At this, the Aquitanians joined Lewis the German in revolt. Lewis the Pious summoned his troops and subdued Aquitaine before marching on Lewis the German, who retreated into the Slavonian marches. Lewis the Pious had crossed the Rhine and barracked his troops at one of the Rhine forts built by his father at the Frank's ford (Frankfurt). His health however, deteriorated, and he died of his consumption aged 62 on mid summer's eve in the year 840AD. His son Lothair was aged 45 and Lewis was aged 36, and a power struggle began between them.

Lewis the German gathered his troops and entered Alamannia, laying siege to Worms. He then went to Saxony to gather support, leaving the siege in the hands of his generals. Lothair came north of the Alps and reached Aix, facing the army of Lewis the German on the River Rhine and Charles the Bald on the River Loire. Lothair, hoping his strong position would cause defections in the opposing armies, agreed a temporary truce. However the Germans were only too eager to throw off the yoke of the Franks whilst the Aquitainians wanted their own king. After further feints, retreats and truces, in June 841AD, the armies of Lewis the German and Charles the Bald had closed together facing Lothair near the River Loire. Pippin was bringing his Aquitainian forces in support of Lothair. Lewis and Charles offered an equitable division of the empire north of the Alps.

Lothair, after drawn out discussions to ensure the arrival of Pippin's army, rejected the offer. The battle at Fontenoy, an area of wooded valleys, commenced on the morning of June 25th. Charles troops were mainly in the valley, with the troops of Lewis in the valley and stretching to the brow of the hill. Lothair moved up to attack Lewis, whilst Pippin moved to engage Charles where most of the slaughter took place. Lothair and Pippin were driven back before fleeing the field.

After so much blood had been spilt and so much division, the fragmented future of the empire was agreed at a treaty made in Verdun in August 843AD. Lewis took the German territories of Saxony, Thuringia, Franconia, Alamannia and Bavaria. Charles took Francia from the River Meuse to the River Loire, plus Aquitaine and Gothia, whilst Lothair took Italy and the territory from the Alps to the German Ocean, being Lotharingia, Provence, and Burgundy.

Much had happened in the empire since Bjorn and Hastein departed for their expedition to the Mediterranean in 863AD. Charles the Great's descendents continued to vie for power against each other, giving no effective defence to the Viking threats. Of Charles the Great's two grandsons still alive whose father was Louis the Pious, Lewis the German was still king of Germany, and Charles the Bald was king of Francia. Lothair I had died in 855AD and been succeeded by his son Lothair II as king of Lotharingia, that kingdom between Germany and Francia, stretching south from the North Sea to Basle. Lothair I's second son, Lewis, was emperor and king of Italy. A third son was Charles king of Provence.

Lewis the emperor and king of Italy, was struggling against an invasion of Saracens and, in 867AD, he besieged them in their fortification at Bari. Finally in 871AD with the help of a Greek fleet they breached the defences and killed most of the defenders. A Frank and Lombard force had also defeated twenty thousand Saracens in the independent Duchy of Beneventum, whose Duke was Adalgis. Adalgis had saved Suliman the Sultan of Bari from death, supposedly for preserving his daughter's chastity whilst she was held as a prisoner in Bari and he took him in as a house prisoner. However the Sultan dissembled the story that Lewis's intention was to take over his Duchy and that of Salerno once the Muslim war was over. This caused Adalgis to seize Lewis and take him prisoner whilst he was in his territory. A great outcry was made that a southern Duchy should be conspiring with the infidels and, with pressure from the Pope, Lewis was released but it damaged his plans to roll back the Saracen invasion. Despite being opposed by Adalgis and his allies along with the Saracens, Lewis still managed to slaughter ten thousand Saracens in 872AD.

During this period Lothair II died in 869AD, and Charles the Bald immediately invaded Lotharingia for territorial gain with an energy and determination he never pursued against the Viking invaders. The Emperor Lewis and king of Italy was too preoccupied with besieging the Saracens in Bari to enforce his legitimate rights to Lotheringia but Lewis the German came with an army to oppose Charles the Bald. At the treaty of Meersen in 870AD, Lewis the German and Charles the Bald, ignoring the rights of the Emperor Lewis, divided Lotheringia between them to form Germany and Francia. The exception was the small kingdom of Provence, ruled by the third son of Lothair I, called Charles, who was epileptic and weak. It had been during Bjorn and Hastein's raid on Arles and Valence, that Charles the Bald had taken the opportunity to invade Provence.

In 875AD, a comet was in the sky throughout the month of June, when The Emperor Lewis and king of Italy died creating great sadness and mourning. He had been a worthy champion, doing more to check the Saracen advances than anything his uncles had achieved in their territories against the Vikings and would most likely have succeeded in unifying Italy had he lived.

Rival factions in Italy supported the camps of Germany and Francia but Lewis the German was now 70 years old, and had left his sons to run the kingdom. His eldest son was Carloman, his second son was Lewis the Saxon named after his Saxon wife and the third son was Charles the Fat, an epileptic and weak-minded son.

Charles the Bald was quick to seize his opportunity by raising an army and, with the support of the Pope, he crossed the Alps and went to Pavia where the Italian council was being convened. The younger son of Lewis the German, Charles the Fat was appointed to further his father's cause and with a small army crossed the Alps into Lombardy. As a sign of things to come however, he retreated back over the Alps as Charles the Bald approached with his army. All was not lost as Lewis the German's eldest and more robust son Carloman arrived with a Bavarian army, smashing through the barriers raised on the mountain passes. Charles the Bald then tried his hand at deception, agreeing to retreat upon Carloman retreating and agreeing to submit his case to arbitration headed by Lewis the German. Such favourable terms persuaded Carloman to accept but once he had retreated, Charles the Bald advanced and went to Rome without opposition, there to have his coronation by the Pope as the Holy Roman Emperor. His estimation of himself now reaching new heights, Charles the Bald took to wearing the long tunics of the Greeks, covered in gold and jewels.

Fresh turmoil was to follow with the death of Lewis the German in August 876AD at the age of seventy-one, a king dedicated to the service of his realm for sixty years. Despite the Pope's appeal for immediate support as the Saracens neared the gates of Rome and, with a Viking fleet of one hundred and twenty ships now coming up the River Seine, Charles the Bald ignored the Pope's pleas and was more interested in taking territory from his dead half brother. He intended to take the whole of Lotheringia up to the River Rhine and so invaded, taking his forces of fifty thousand men to Cologne overlooking the River Rhine.

On his death, Lewis the German's kingdom was split three ways. His elder son Carloman took the East Mark, Bavaria and Corinthia. Lewis the Saxon took Saxony, the Danish Mark, Thuringia and eastern Lorraine, whilst Charles the Fat took Swabia and Alsace. Lewis the Saxon alone opposed his uncle, bringing his forces to Deutz in early October, a camp on the opposite banks of the River Rhine to his uncle at Cologne. Lewis could not safely cross into the disputed territory but realised he had no alternative but to fight his uncle. Leaving his campfires burning, Lewis stole away south with his army in the night and crossed the River Rhine between Koblenz and Andernach where he took up a strong position in the hills. On hearing of this, Charles the Bald broke camp and, with his customary deception, sent word that he was ready to discuss a peace treaty to which Lewis agreed. Lewis then released half his army to seek provisions whereupon Charles the Bald immediately marched his full army to attack Lewis. Lewis however was forewarned by the Archbishop of Cologne and further aided by the local guides who supported him. They led Charles the Bald's army on a merry dance through the hills, taking a day to cover fifteen miles, marching through the night in torrential rain and arriving exhausted in the morning. Lewis's forces were no less uncomfortable, standing guard and prepared for a night attack, with Lewis ordering that all his men should wear white garb to identify themselves in the dark. The first attack fell upon the Saxons who were driven back but the Franks came to their support and rescued the situation. In the fighting two Counts leading Charles the Bald's forces were killed. The forces of Charles the Bald began to lose heart, finding they had not surprised Lewis as expected and now faced with a hard fight after a long night's march, they fell back and eventually panicked. Charles the Bald, never at the front of his forces, fled for his life to Liege. Charles had installed his young second wife Richildis well away from the battle at Herstal where he expected her to deliver the good news of his success. She in turn was forced to flee, and being heavily pregnant, gave birth prematurely to a boy who died. Thus we see Andernach as the first major battle between Germany and Francia.

Charles the Bald paid five thousand pounds of silver to the Viking fleet on the Seine without a fight, but he did agree to support the Pope when he met the bishops at Ravenna and was re-elected emperor after his defeat by Lewis the Saxon. However Lewis the German's oldest son Carloman decided to challenge him by marching over the Brenner Pass. Charles appealed for reinforcements to be sent but none were despatched, forcing him to retreat. Fate then took a hand when Carloman contracted a disease that caused paralysis. His brother Lewis the Saxon took control of his territories but he too was not long to reign before he died, leaving the remaining brother, Charles the Fat, as the successor. Charles the Bald also contracted a fever and died in October 877AD at the age of fifty-three. Lewis the Stammerer succeeded Charles who then lent support to Abbot Hugh on an expedition against the Loire Vikings. However, his reign only lasted a short time and he died in April 879AD.

With Lewis the Stammerer's younger brother, Charles King of Acquitaine, accidentally killed whilst out hunting and, with the other brothers Lothair in a monastery and Carloman blinded by his father, Lewis the Stammerer's young sons and heirs, Lewis the Elder, Carloman and Charles the Simple, were about to be disinherited. Conrad of Paris and Abbot Gozlin offered the crown to Lewis the Saxon, who then brought his army into the field. Hugo the Abbot of Tours, and Boso the brother of Richildis and brother in law of Charles the Bald opposed the offer and Lewis the Saxon was forced to come to terms whereby he now took over the whole of Lotheringia. Before his death, the elderly Charles the Bald under the undue influence of his young wife, had previously indulged Boso's ambitions, and now Boso had himself proclaimed king of Provence and Burgundy with the support of the bishops - the first non-Carling king in the empire.

It was now in the year 880AD, that two Danish kings Godfred and Siegfred arrived intent on conquest, ravaging widely in both the German territories and in Francia. Lewis the Saxon had a superior force when he met a body of Godfred's men between the Rivers Scheldt and Meuse. The Danes were defeated but Lewis the Saxon's son, Hugo, who had been leading his men into battle, had been wounded and was carried off by the Danes as they retreated to a farm at Thuin on the River Sambre, a tributary of the River Meuse. This caused Lewis to hold back in attacking the farm in the hope of negotiating a ransom. He watched the Danes' camp fires burning during the night, only to discover the next morning that the Danes had departed to their fleet leaving the dead body of his son on the ground and that the fires had been those cremating the bodies of nearly five thousand dead Danes. Shortly afterwards the Danes were on the River Elbe and met a Saxon army led by Duke Bruno on the Luneburg Heath. Here Duke Bruno was killed and his army decimated.

By 881AD, the lands between the Rivers Scheldt and the Somme had been ravaged leaving little profit remaining for the Danes, who then looked south. There was however one outstanding victory for Francia, when Lewis the Stammerer's son, Lewis the Elder, raised an army to confront the Danes on the Somme. Leading his men from the front, Lewis the Elder won an outstanding victory against the Danes at Saucourt, killing some eight thousand Danes. This was a victory against the Vikings that his grandfather Charles the Bald could never equal.

Checked in Francia, the Danes moved on in force to Germany, with the combined great armies of Godfred and Siegfred poised for conquest. Germany was then more vulnerable as Lewis the Saxon was ill, declining in health since the death of his son Hugo. His paralysed brother Carloman had died some two years earlier and Lewis the Saxon had succeeded him in Bavaria and the East Mark. The sole remaining brother, Charles the Fat went to Italy to claim the title of emperor. Carloman left behind an illegitimate son called Arnulf, who ruled under Lewis the Saxon as king of Carinthia and who was to achieve greater things.

The Danes spread out over the lower River Rhine, plundering widely before moving south to sack Cologne and destroy its churches. The same fate followed at Neuss and Bonn, before taking the imperial palace of Charles the Great at Aix la Chapelle (Aachen) with ease. Finally the threat made by Gothfrith the Danish king came to pass some seventy years after it had been made. They burnt part of the palace and used the churches built by Charles the Great to stall their horses in the aisles. From Aachen the Danes travelled fifty miles south to the Abbey at Prum where they celebrated their festival of Midvintersblot on January 14th, over a period of three days. Ironically the celebrated festival was the one that called for peace and a good harvest. They then returned to a fortified royal palace at Elsloo near Maastricht some twenty miles from Aix la Chapelle.

It was at this time in 882AD that the Danes, encouraged by the death of Lewis the Saxon and his succession by the weak Charles the Fat to his kingdom of Germany and Lotheringia, moved south to the country around the River Mosel and sacked Treves (Trier), whilst the Christians fled and sheltered in Mainz to the east. On hearing that Charles the Fat had raised a large army returning from Italy with the Lombards alongside the Saxons, the Franks, the Frisians, the Swabians, and the Bavarians under Arnulf; the Danes, always with good intelligence, retreated back to Elsloo. Charles the Fat besieged Elsloo in July 882AD, only to be met with a hail of large stones fired from the fortification. In fact the missiles did more to damage the walls of the Danes own defences but it had its desired effect on the easily intimidated Charles the Fat.

The Danes had no provisions and were in a weak position but, true to his character, Charles the Fat opened negotiations, instead of taking advantage of those strengths he possessed and which were most often created by others. The Danes then opened the gates, putting a shield on the wall as a sign of peace. All manner of traders entered to barter for the treasures they had plundered. The Danes then closed the gates and killed all the traders within, taking their possessions. Despite such gross treachery Charles the Fat paid two thousand seven hundred pounds of silver and gave away territory on the Rivers Rhine and Waal. This was conditional upon Godfred becoming a Christian and defending Frisia against the Vikings. Godfred took the territory but had other ambitions. He married Gisella, the sister of Hugh of Lorraine who acted as a tyrant and had his own ambitions. He and his sister were the illegitimate descendents of Lothair II who together planned to take German territory with Hugh of Lorraine fronting the move and with Godfred to be the power behind the throne.

The Danes who had chosen not to settle in the lands offered by Godfred took their share of Charles' silver and sailed to Francia with Siegfred. There they posed a great threat to the whole of the kingdom. At this time in 882AD, Lewis the Stammerer's oldest and more able son, Lewis the Elder, died in an unfortunate accident. The worse for wear through drink, he was pursuing a young girl romantically, who chose to flee to her father's house. Riding his horse through a low archway, his reactions were too slow to avoid hitting the stonework with his shoulder. The injuries sustained from this and from the fall caused his death. Francia, then under grave threat, was now in the hands of a young King Carloman who was soon to die in 884AD, meeting a similar fate to his uncle, King Charles of Acquitaine, killed accidentally on a hunting trip by a companion called Berhthold. It was put out that he was killed by a wild boar to protect Berhthold from reprisal. His successor was his younger brother a boy of five years of age, Charles the Simple, under the guidance of Abbot Hugh. In such circumstances Charles the Fat then took over the whole of the empire once ruled by Charles the Great, an area his limited capabilities could not effectively govern. Charles the Simple served as an under king. The one exception was the territory of Bergundy, still independently controlled by Boso the non-Carling king.

In 883AD a new body of Vikings comprising many from Francia came to the lower River Rhine but, despite his agreement with Charles to defend the region, Godfred offered no opposition. They camped at Duisburg at the confluence of the Rivers Rhine and Ruhr, which greatly alarmed Charles the Fat and his advisors. Godfred moved his plans to expand his territory forward. Ready to march his army, he demanded new territories in the wine areas around the River Mosel north from Koblenz to Andernach and Bonn in 885AD. He was also in communication with a new Viking fleet about to move into Saxony from the River Elbe and into the mouth of the River Alar.

All could see that the demand would put a spear into the very heart of the German kingdom, opening up the chance for total conquest of the empire. Finally on the advice of Duke Henry, it was agreed to use some unchristian tactics, and Godfred was invited to discuss his demands at a meeting in his territory attended by Count Everard (a man already divested of his lands by Godfred), and Willibert the Archbishop of Cologne who was unaware of any treacherous plans. The meeting took place on the Batavian island where the River Waal separates from the River Rhine. The meeting started without rancour exploring the options arising from Godfred's demands, thus creating a relaxed and trusting atmosphere. It was then agreed that Archbishop Willibert should be sent to escort Godfred's wife Gisella to the meeting so she could act as a mediator. Before she arrived, a second meeting was arranged, at which Godfred and his attendants were unarmed and devoid of suspicion, never thinking that Christians could also be treacherous. A quarrel was manufactured and in the heated exchange, Count Everard killed Godfred with his sword and the attendant Danes were massacred. As for Hugh of Lorraine, he was arrested at Gondreville where a meeting had been simultaneously arranged.

Meanwhile, the Danes who had come over from Francia, had landed at Norden near the estuary of the River Alar. Rimbert the Archbishop of Bremen who had been a Danish boy slave purchased by the Christians to help convert the Danes under Anscar, rallied a local army of Frisians to oppose the Danes. He was not involved in the subsequent fighting but sat on a hill praying for their victory. The victory was decisive for the Frisians. Nearly ten thousand Vikings were killed. The Danish fleet on the River Elbe however had moved east into Saxony. The Saxon army was able to keep them in check. The Saxons then had the good fortune to see the Frisians arrive on the river with a large fleet, thus trapping the Vikings between two armies. The Vikings were decisively beaten and so, with the death of Godfred, the threat to the German part of the empire peaked and declined thereafter. The position in Francia however was not so benign. Siegfred was also bent on conquest.

When Siegfred left Germany with his danegeld in 882AD he first went to the River Scheld sailing up to Conde where he made camp. From this base they moved through the extensive forests to the west of the River Meuse until they came to Laon, some thirty miles north of Rheims. They could not assail it as the city was built on a rock. They then moved south to the city of Rheims itself where the walls had fallen into decay and had not been repaired. Despite its vulnerable situation, the Danes did not enter the city, fearing a trap. Bands of Danes were roaming widely and were intercepted by the larger forces of Abbot Hugh. Eventually Siegfred retreated back to his camp at Conde. From here in the winter of 882/83AD, they ravaged widely as far west as the River Somme where the young Carloman, the recent successor to Lewis the Elder, and Abbot Hugh had placed their forces. They did not engage the Danes and fell back to Amiens. The local nobility saw that they could no longer rely on the king. Instead of confronting the Danes they offered a colossal twelve thousand pounds of silver. The Danes took hostages whilst it was being collected. Half the payment was made at Amiens in 884AD. Part of the fleet then sailed to Rochester in England and part to Germany and the Rivers Alar and the Elbe. Following reverses in England and Germany in 884AD, they returned to Louvain (Leuven) in Belgium where many had settled. Hearing of the accidental hunting death of Carloman, they killed their hostages, broke their treaty and marched into Francia. The nobility who were still raising the other half of the twelve thousand pounds of silver protested bitterly but received the reply that the Danes agreement was to leave King Carloman in peace. Now that he was dead they could not disturb his peace.

Charles the Fat was still in Italy after being offered his new crown as the Holy Roman Emperor by Hugo of Tours. Returning from Italy, Charles the Fat raised an army from Lotheringia to confront the Danes from Louvain but he would not take command and, with no capable leaders, the army drifted away.

Siegfred now decided to move to the heart of France, taking his fleet into the River Seine, first attacking and plundering Rouen in July 885AD. Local resistance was given under Count Reginald but, when he was killed, the army fled in panic. Siegfred then moved upstream to Paris, which had been better fortified by Charles the Bald with two bridges supported by stone pillars to block river access. Paris was then a city on an island, with the river flowing by to the north and south of the island. One bridge connected the north bank to the city, and the other connected the south bank. The emperor, Charles the Fat was on the River Danube as far away as he could be before moving back to Italy, leaving the Parisians in fear as some forty thousand Danes approached with their huge fleet.

Defence was organised by Bishop Gozlin and Odo the Count of Paris and the eldest son of Robert the Strong whose qualities he inherited. Robert the Strong, we may recall, had been killed by Hastein's men when he returned from his Mediterranean voyage with Bjorn. Bishop Gozlin and Odo had quickly erected a large wooden tower on the north bridge to defend it and to prevent access to the city walls.

Siegfred tried first to negotiate a safe passage upstream, saying that he would not attack Paris if the Parisians allowed access through the bridges. However, Gozlin and Odo did not believe him and rejected the offer and so the siege began on November 26th 885AD, beginning at the north bridge.

The tower was fully completed and was defended by some two hundred men. It was attacked using lead ball and stone missiles, battering rams, and attempts were made to undermine the structure. The defenders took a heavy toll of the Danes, using their bows to good effect and pouring boiling oil and pitch on to them causing many to jump into the water. The Danes had their women with them who would jeer if at any time the attackers fell back. During the night the Parisians strengthened the tower and built it higher. On the second day the Danes used wooden houses on wheels with the roof covered in skins, to protect themselves from the arrows but the boiling oil and pitch took its toll. The defenders also began to use missiles effectively against the Danes. The Danes managed to undermine one of the walls of the tower and set it on fire but, though the structure moved, it did not fall. They then set huge fires alight next to the tower's walls that showed every sign of success but a heavy rain extinguished the fires.

Siegfred then reassessed his tactics and decided to prepare for a long winter siege. He established a fortified camp and sent out his mounted men on forays over large distances to provide provisions for the winter, plundering at will. Messages had been sent to Charles the Fat to come to the aid of Paris but he showed no signs of acting. By the end of January 886AD, Siegfred was ready to act again, having constructed more wheeled vehicles to protect larger numbers of men. The battering rams were now brought to bear against the tower. There was a ditch between the bridge and the city walls, which the Danes tried to fill in with branches, dead animals and the bodies of their prisoners. They then prepared three fire ships to burn the wooden structure of the bridge, but the ships drifted into the stone pillars and had little effect. Nature now came to the aid of the Danes as the winter rains raised the level of the river and swept away part of the bridge in early February. This cut off the tower from the city and the Danes then successfully set fire to it before killing all those remaining therein. Access to the city from the north bridge was now impossible. The Danes moved to the south bridge and set up camp at the Abbey of Saint Germain des Pres but no progress was made against the south bridge either. Siegfred then offered to end his part of the siege on payment of a small sum for his forces, a mere sixty pounds of silver. At this time Bishop Gozlin and Abbot Hugh died, depressing the spirits of the Parisians and pestilence broke out in the city. Odo now became commander of the Parisian forces. He resolved to break out and seek the Emperor Charles the Fat, to urge him to come to the relief of Paris. Siegfred meanwhile had received the danegeld, and departed in April with part of the fleet, but the bulk of the Danes stayed to continue the siege under Sinrik who resolved one day to camp at the head of the River Seine.

Odo eventually returned with an army but without Charles the Fat. The Danes sought to prevent them entering Paris. However a force from Paris opened up a front from the rear that enabled him to break through. Charles the Fat finally collected an army and slowly made his way to Paris. It was now August, and Charles sent forward Duke Henry to face the initial onslaught, whilst he stayed sixty miles away at Laon. Duke Henry arrived and camped at Montmartre. The Danes responded by strengthening their defences putting up their palisades and digging ditches. They in their turn were now besieged. At the head of his men Duke Henry rode forward and fell into a ditch the Danes had covered with branches and leaves and was promptly speared to death. His men lost heart and retreated. Sinric died, having the misfortune to drown in the river but the Danes, never lacking in determination, attacked Paris again although the defenders stood firm.

Charles the Fat sent forward a force of six hundred Franks to reinforce the garrison in Paris and they managed to enter the city. Charles the Fat finally arrived with his army to camp at Montmartre in September. With the Danes confined to their camp, Paris was open to access thanks to the stout defence put up by its defenders. It was now the turn of Charles the Fat to undo the gains the Parisians had made, which had stalled the Danes plans for the conquest of Francia, an opportunity that would have opened up on the fall of Paris.

With the Danes in their camp facing a vast army greatly outnumbering them, Charles the Fat did nothing over the next month until spurred to panic when he heard that Siegfred had entered the Seine with a new army and fleet. He offered the Danes seven hundred pounds of silver to leave Paris, and gave them leave to go up the River Seine and into Burgundy where they would be free to ravage at will. Burgundy was under the control of King Boso, the self-proclaimed king. The decision to allow the Vikings into Christian Burgundy was therefore partly revenge against a non-Carling king.

By now the various regions could see that the vast empire led by a weak man could never serve their interests, compared to the protection of a strong local leader. In November 887AD, Charles the

Fat was to attend a legislative assembly at Trebur, prior to which political manoeuvres had taken place to undermine Charles and bring about his downfall. Once at Trebur, Arnulf Duke of Carinthia and the natural if illegitimate son of Carloman and grandson of Lewis the German marched with his army against Charles the Fat. Charles had no support and was abandoned by all. Arnulf became king of Germany, a country now divorced from the Latin speaking parts of the empire. By January 888AD Charles the Fat, now abandoned by his wife and mentally infirm, was dead. Odo, Count of Paris, the commander of the Paris garrison, and descendent of Robert the Strong, was made the non-Carling king of Francia. So ended the Holy Roman Empire with the death of Charles the Great's great grandson.

In the spring of 888AD, the Danes returned to Paris to collect their danegeld, having ravaged Burgundy for a year. The silver was paid over conditional upon their leaving Francia but they managed to slip past Paris into the upper Seine. They were stopped from reaching their objective but did get into the River Marne, and plundered the territory up to Germany. Had Godfred been successful in acquiring the lands around the River Mosel, the two great Danish armies could have united to take the whole of the empire but the zenith of the Danes opportunities had now passed never to return.

The Carloman House of Charles the Great had, through the moral weaknesses of his grandsons and great grandsons, lost forever the Holy Roman Empire, and almost lost Christian Europe. It was, however, the ambitions and actions of Charles the Great that had caused the fiery spirit of revenge amongst a vigorous and proud seafaring people, revenge that later developed into a way of life, colonisation and settlement. In the end their conversion to Christianity was through the wise words and example of peaceful people and not through the point of a spear.

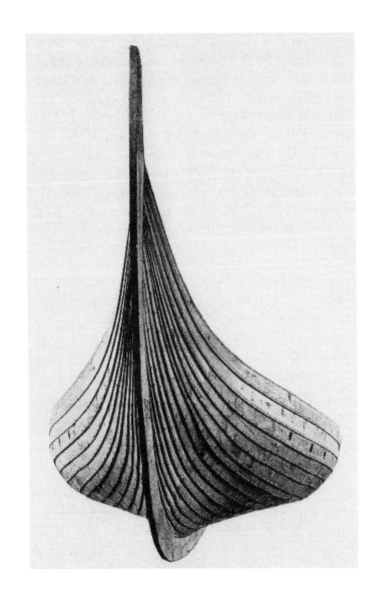

THE GOKSTAD SHIP BURIAL OF OLAFR THE WHITE

COURTESY OF OSLO SHIP MUSEUM

THE GOKSTAD SHIP BURIAL OF OLAFR THE WHITE

COURTESY OF OSLO SHIP MUSEUM

THE GOKSTAD SHIP BURIAL OF OLAFR THE WHITE

COURTESY OF OSLO SHIP MUSEUM

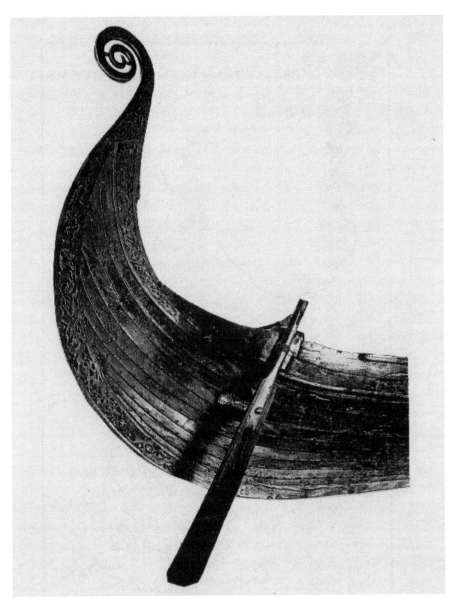

THE OSEBERG SHIP BURIAL OF QUEEN ASA

COURTESY OF OSLO SHIP MUSEUM

175

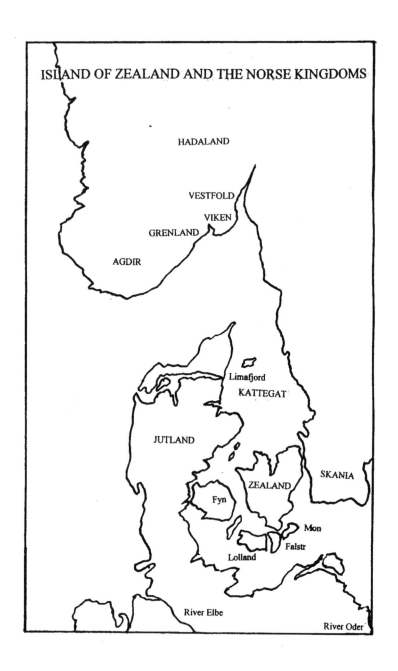

ISLAND OF ZEALAND AND THE NORSE KINGDOMS

HADALAND

VESTFOLD

VIKEN

GRENLAND

AGDIR

Limafjord

KATTEGAT

JUTLAND

SKANIA

ZEALAND

Fyn

Mon

Falstr

Lolland

River Elbe

River Oder

KINGDOMS OF THE ANGLO SAXONS, THE PICTS, SCOTS, BRITONS AND NORSE SETTLEMENTS

Shetland Is

Orkney Is
Cape Wrath
Pentland Firth
CAITHNESS
SUTHER-
LAND
OUTER HEBRIDES
MORAY
GAILL GAEDHIL
PICTLAND
Firth of Forth
DAL RIADA
River Clyde
BERNICIA
STRATHCLYDE
BRITONS
NORTHUMBERLAND
Isle of Man
DEIRA
Isle of Anglesey
Dublin
MERCIA
EAST
ANGLIA
WESSEX
KENT

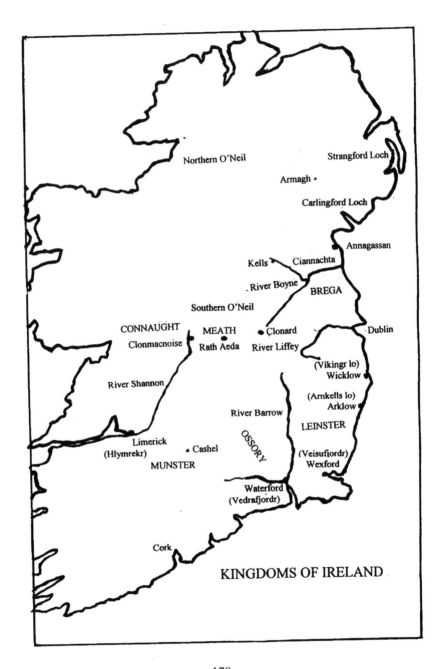

Northern O'Neil

Strangford Loch

Armagh •

Carlingford Loch

Annagassan

Kells •   Ciannachta

. River Boyne

BREGA

Southern O'Neil

CONNAUGHT   MEATH   • Clonard   Dublin

Clonmacnoise   • Rath Aeda   River Liffey

(Vikingr lo)
Wicklow •

River Shannon

(Arnkells lo)
Arklow •

River Barrow

LEINSTER

Limerick   OSSORY
(Hlymrekr)   • Cashel

MUNSTER   (Veisufiordr)
Wexford

Waterford
(Vedrafjordr)

Cork

KINGDOMS OF IRELAND

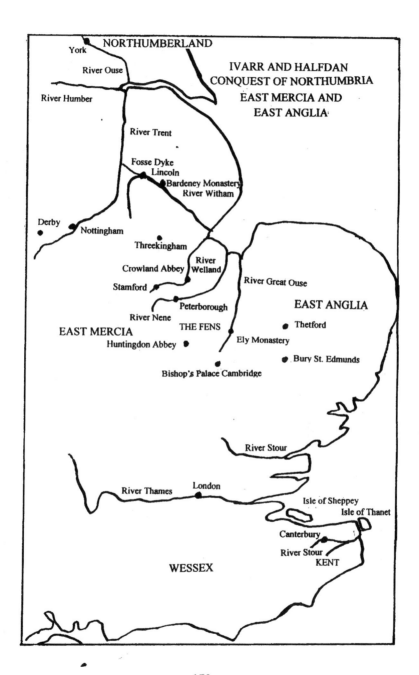

IVARR AND HALFDAN
CONQUEST OF NORTHUMBRIA
EAST MERCIA AND
EAST ANGLIA

NORTHUMBERLAND
York
River Ouse
River Humber
River Trent
Fosse Dyke
Lincoln
Bardeney Monastery
River Witham
Derby
Nottingham
Threekingham
River
Welland
Crowland Abbey
Stamford
River Great Ouse
EAST ANGLIA
Thetford
Peterborough
River Nene
THE FENS
EAST MERCIA
Huntingdon Abbey
Ely Monastery
Bury St. Edmunds
Bishop's Palace Cambridge
River Stour
River Thames
London
Isle of Sheppey
Isle of Thanet
Canterbury
River Stour
KENT
WESSEX

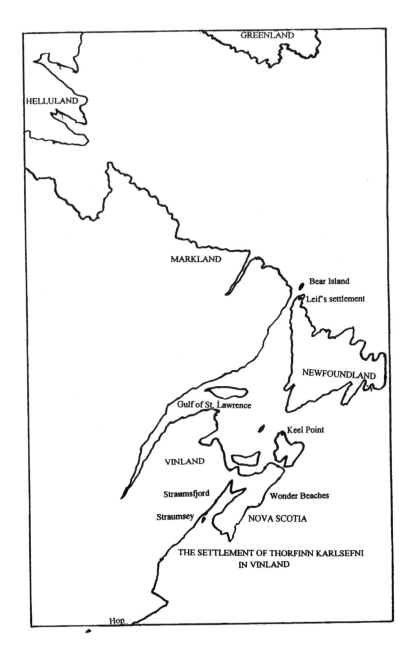

GREENLAND

HELLULAND

MARKLAND

Bear Island

Leif's settlement

NEWFOUNDLAND

Gulf of St. Lawrence

Keel Point

VINLAND

Straumsfjord

Wonder Beaches

Straumsey

NOVA SCOTIA

THE SETTLEMENT OF THORFINN KARLSEFNI
IN VINLAND

Hop

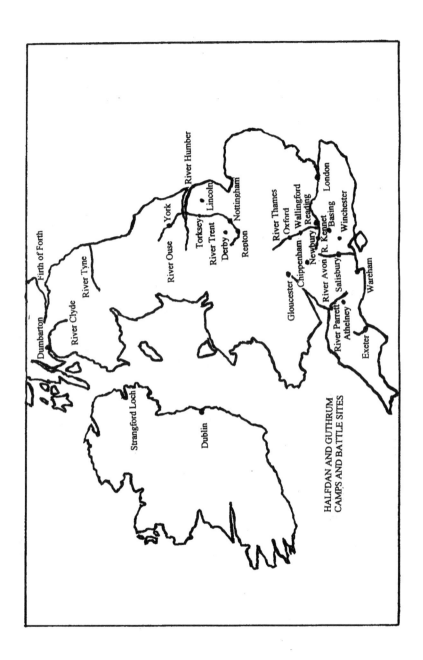

HALFDAN AND GUTHRUM
CAMPS AND BATTLE SITES

Firth of Forth
Dumbarton
River Clyde
River Tyne
River Ouse
York
River Humber
Torksey
Lincoln
River Trent
Derby
Nottingham
Repton
Strangford Loch
Dublin
Gloucester
Chippenham
River Avon
Athelney
River Parrett
Salisbury
Exeter
Wareham
River Thames
Oxford
Wallingford
Reading
Newbury
R. Kennet
Basing
Winchester
London

181

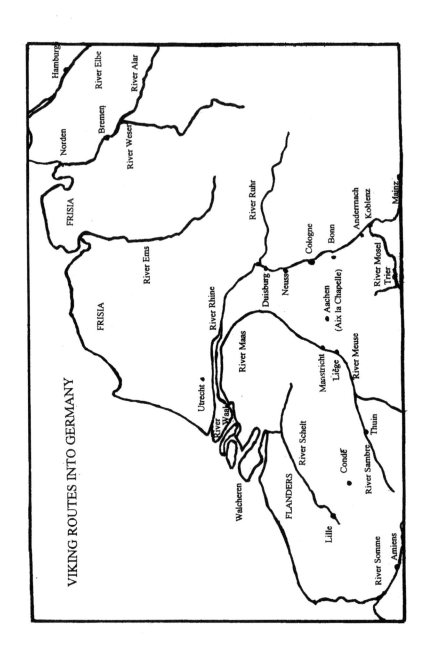

VIKING ROUTES INTO GERMANY

Hamburg
River Elbe
River Alar
Bremen
Norden
River Weser
FRISIA
River Ruhr
Andernach
Koblenz
Mainz
Cologne
Bonn
River Ems
River Mosel
Trier
Duisburg
Neuss
FRISIA
River Rhine
Aachen
(Aix la Chapelle)
River Maas
Utrecht
River Waal
River Meuse
Maastricht
Liège
River Scheit
Walcheren
Thuin
FLANDERS
Condé
Lille
River Sambre
River Somme
Amiens

182

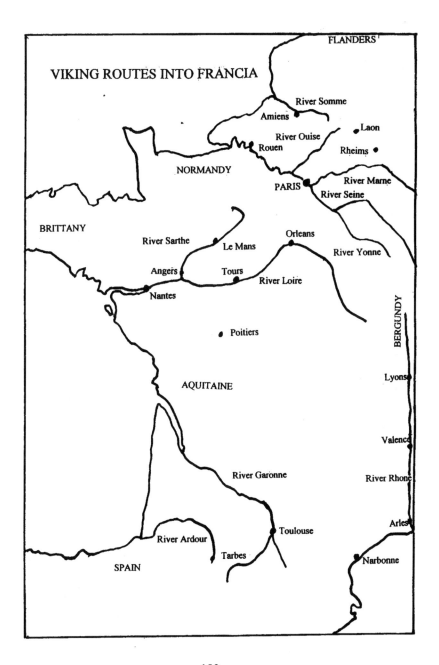

VIKING ROUTES INTO FRANCIA

FLANDERS

River Somme

Amiens

Laon

River Ouise

Rouen

Rheims

NORMANDY

River Marne

PARIS

River Seine

BRITTANY

River Sarthe

Le Mans

Orleans

River Yonne

Angers

Tours

River Loire

Nantes

Poitiers

BERGUNDY

AQUITAINE

Lyons

Valence

River Garonne

River Rhone

River Ardour

Toulouse

Arles

Tarbes

Narbonne

SPAIN

183

THE HOLY ROMAN EMPIRE – THE HOUSE OF CARLING

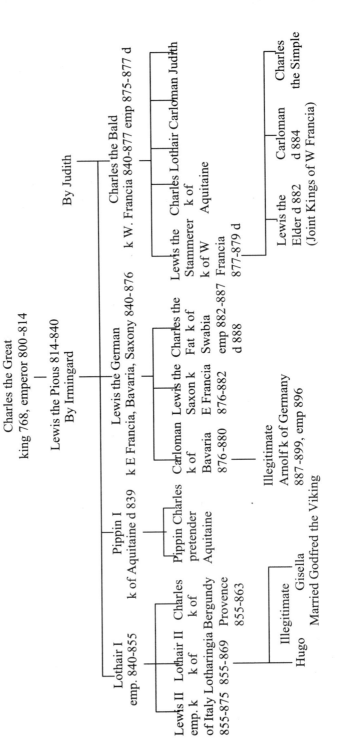

Charles the Great
king 768, emperor 800-814

Lewis the Pious 814-840
By Irmingard

By Judith

Lothair I
emp. 840-855

Lewis the German
k E Francia, Bavaria, Saxony 840-876

Charles the Bald
k W. Francia 840-877 emp 875-877 d

Pippin I
k of Aquitaine d 839

Lewis II
emp. k
of Italy
855-875

Lothair II
k of
Lotharingia
855-869

Charles
k of
Bergundy
Provence
855-863

Pippin
pretender

Charles
k of
Aquitaine

Carloman
k of
Bavaria
876-880

Lewis the
Saxon k
E Francia
876-882

Charles the
Fat k of
Swabia
emp 882-887
d 888

Lewis the
Stammerer
k of W
Francia
877-879 d

Charles Lothair Carloman Judith
k of
Aquitaine

Illegitimate
Arnolf k of Germany
887-899, emp 896

Illegitimate
Hugo

Gisella
Married Godfred the Viking

Lewis the
Elder d 882

Carloman
d 884

Charles
the Simple

(Joint Kings of W Francia)